THE $ SMART COOK

General manager *Christine Whiston*
Editorial director *Susan Tomnay*
Creative director & designer *Hieu Chi Nguyen*
Senior editor *Stephanie Kistner*
Extra text *Lynn Bryan*
Food director *Pamela Clark*
Food editor *Cathie Lonnie*

Director of sales *Brian Cearnes*
Marketing manager *Bridget Cody*
Communications & brand manager *Xanthe Roberts*
Senior business analyst *Rebecca Varela*
Circulation manager *Jarna Mclean*
Operations manager *David Scotto*
Production manager *Victoria Jefferys*
European rights enquiries *Laura Bamford lbamford@acpuk.com*

ACP Books are published by ACP Magazines a division of PBL Media Pty Limited

Group publishing & sales director, Women's lifestyle *Lynette Phillips*
Group editorial director, Women's lifestyle *Pat Ingram*
Commercial manager, Women's lifestyle *Seymour Cohen*
Marketing director, Women's lifestyle *Matthew Dominello*
Research Director, Women's lifestyle *Justin Stone*
PBL Media, Chief Executive Officer *Ian Law*

Produced by ACP Books, Sydney. Published by ACP Books, a division of ACP Magazines Ltd.
54 Park St, Sydney NSW Australia 2000. GPO Box 4088, Sydney, NSW 2001.
Phone +61 2 9282 8618 Fax +61 2 9267 9438
acpbooks@acpmagazines.com.au www.acpbooks.com.au

Printed by C&C Offset Printing, China.

Australia Distributed by Network Services, GPO Box 4088, Sydney, NSW 2001.
Phone +61 2 9282 8777 Fax +61 2 9264 3278 networkweb@networkservicescompany.com.au
United Kingdom Distributed by Australian Consolidated Press (UK),
10 Scirocco Close, Moulton Park Office Village, Northampton, NN3 6AP.
Phone +44 1604 642 200 Fax +44 1604 642 300 books@acpuk.com www.acpuk.com
Canada Distributed by Publishers Group Cananda,
Order Desk & Customer Service, 9050 Shaughnessy Street, Vancouver, BC V6P 6E5.
Phone (800) 663 5714 Fax (800) 565 3770 service@raincoast.com
New Zealand Distributed by Southern Publishers Group, 21 Newton Road, Auckland, NZ.
Phone +64 9 360 0692 Fax +64 9 360 0695 hub@spg.co.nz
South Africa Distributed by PSD Promotions, 30 Diesel Road Isando, Gauteng Johannesburg.
PO Box 1175, Isando 1600, Gauteng Johannesburg.
Phone +27 11 392 6065/6/7 Fax +27 11 392 6079/80 orders@psdprom.co.za

Author: Clark, Pamela
Title: The $ smart cook / Pamela Clark
ISBN: 978-1-86396-926-0 (pbk)
Notes: Includes index
Subjects: Low budget cookery. Cookery.
Dewey number: 641.552

© ACP Magazines Ltd 2009
ABN 18 053 273 546

Cover *Shepherd's pie*, page 132
Photographer *Dean Wilmot*
Stylist *Louise Bickle*
Food preparation *Nick Banbury*

The publisher would like to thank No Chintz, Dandi and Mark Conway for props used in photography.

Photographers *Alan Benson, Steve Brown, Joshua Dasey, Rowan Fotheringham, Louise Lister, Andre Martin, Rob Palmer,
Stuart Scott, George Seper, Brett Stevens, John Paul Urizar, Ian Wallace, Dean Wilmot, Gorta Yuuki, Tanya Zouev.*
Stylists *Wendy Berecry, Julz Beresford, Kristin Beusing, Alexia Biggs, Margot Braddon, Kate Brown,
Rachel Brown, Marie-Helene Clauzon, Jane Hann, Michaela Le Compte, Vicki Liley, David Morgan,
Kate Nixon, Sarah O'Brien, Justine Osborne, Louise Pickford, Stephanie Souvlis.*

To order books, phone 136 116 (within Australia) or online at www.acpbooks.com.au
Send recipe enquiries to: recipeenquiries@acpmagazines.com.au

THE AUSTRALIAN
Women's Weekly

THE $ SMART COOK

acp
books

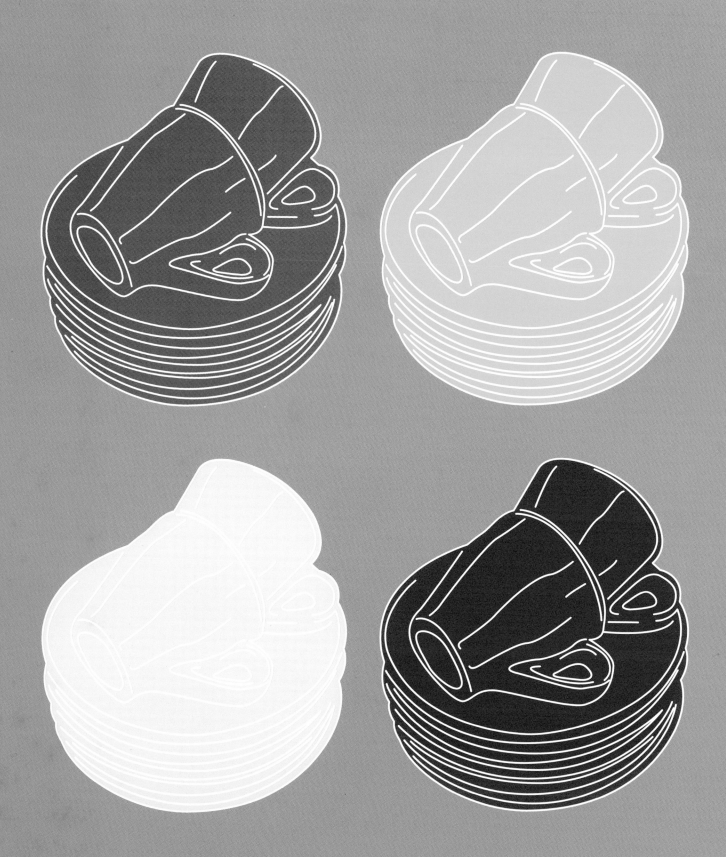

contents

soup

vegetable soup

You need approximately 1kg of untrimmed silver beet for this recipe.

1 tablespoon vegetable oil
2 large brown onions (400g), chopped finely
2 large carrots (360g), chopped coarsely
8 trimmed celery stalks (800g), chopped coarsely
3 cloves garlic, crushed
1 litre (4 cups) vegetable stock
1 litre (4 cups) water
¾ cup (165g) soup pasta
2 medium zucchini (240g), sliced thickly
250g trimmed silver beet, chopped coarsely

1 Heat oil in large saucepan; cook onion, carrot, celery and garlic, stirring, until vegetables soften.
2 Add stock and the water; bring to the boil. Reduce heat; simmer, uncovered, 10 minutes. Add pasta and zucchini; simmer, uncovered, stirring occasionally, about 5 minutes or until pasta is tender. Add silver beet; cook, stirring, until silver beet just wilts.

prep + cook time **50 minutes**   serves **4**
nutritional count per serving   **6.8g total fat (1.2g saturated fat); 1296kJ (310 cal); 43.5g carbohydrate; 12.4g protein; 11.5g fibre**

Parsley will keep in the freezer. Use what you need from the fresh bunch, then wash and dry the remainder; chop finely, and freeze in a small plastic container.

lentil soup

1 tablespoon olive oil
3 rindless bacon rashers (195g), chopped coarsely
1 medium brown onion (150g), chopped finely
1 medium carrot (120g), chopped finely
1 trimmed celery stalk (100g), chopped finely
1 cup (200g) brown lentils
410g can crushed tomatoes
1 litre (4 cups) chicken stock
1 bay leaf
¼ cup coarsely chopped fresh flat-leaf parsley

1 Heat oil in large saucepan; cook bacon, onion, carrot and celery, stirring, until onion softens.
2 Add lentils, undrained tomatoes, stock and bay leaf; bring to the boil. Reduce heat; simmer, covered, 30 minutes.
3 Discard bay leaf; serve soup sprinkled with parsley.
prep + cook time *1 hour* **serves** *4*
nutritional count per serving *13.4g total fat (3.7g saturated fat); 1484kJ (355 cal); 27.8g carbohydrate; 26.1g protein; 10.1g fibre*

scotch broth

2.25 litres (9 cups) water
1kg lamb neck chops
¾ cup (150g) barley
1 large brown onion (200g), chopped coarsely
2 medium carrots (240g), chopped coarsely
1 medium leek (350g), sliced thinly
2 cups (160g) finely shredded savoy cabbage
½ cup (60g) frozen peas
2 tablespoons finely chopped fresh flat-leaf parsley

1 Combine the water in large saucepan with lamb and barley; bring to the boil. Reduce heat; simmer, covered, 1 hour, skimming fat from surface occasionally. Add onion, carrot and leek; simmer, covered, about 30 minutes, or until carrot is tender.
2 Remove lamb from pan. When cool enough to handle, remove and discard bones; shred lamb meat coarsely.
3 Return lamb to soup with cabbage and peas; cook, uncovered, about 10 minutes or until peas are tender.
4 Serve soup sprinkled with parsley.

prep + cook time *2 hours 15 minutes* serves *4*
nutritional count per serving *24.4g total fat
(10.7g saturated fat); 2274kJ (544 cal); 32.8g
carbohydrate; 43.2g protein; 10.7g fibre*

Freshly squeezed lemon juice can be
frozen in an ice-cube tray for easy access.

soupe au pistou

1 tablespoon olive oil
1 small brown onion (80g), chopped finely
2 cloves garlic, sliced thinly
1 large carrot (180g), chopped finely
1 trimmed celery stalk (100g), chopped finely
1 medium potato (200g), cut into 1cm cubes
⅓ cup (75g) risoni
3 cups (750ml) chicken stock
1 cup (250ml) water
400g can white beans, rinsed, drained
2 tablespoons lemon juice
⅓ cup (90g) basil pesto

1 Heat oil in large saucepan, add onion, garlic,
carrot and celery; cook, stirring, until onion softens.
Add potato, risoni, stock and the water; bring to
the boil. Reduce heat; cook about 10 minutes or
until risoni is tender.
2 Stir in beans; cook, uncovered, 1 minute.
3 Remove pan from heat; stir in juice. Serve with
basil pesto. Accompany with fresh, crusty white
bread, if you like.
prep + cook time *35 minutes*   serves *4*
nutritional count per serving *14.8g total fat
(3g saturated fat); 1342kJ (321 cal); 31.4g
carbohydrate; 12g protein; 7.5g fibre*

fish chowder

40g butter
1 large brown onion (200g), chopped coarsely
1 clove garlic, crushed
2 rindless bacon rashers (130g), chopped coarsely
2 tablespoons plain flour
2 medium potatoes (400g), chopped coarsely
3 cups (750ml) milk
2 cups (500ml) vegetable stock
400g firm white fish fillets, chopped coarsely
2 tablespoons finely chopped fresh chives

1 Melt butter in large saucepan; cook onion, garlic and bacon, stirring, until onion softens.
2 Add flour to pan; cook, stirring, 1 minute. Add potato, milk and stock; bring to the boil. Reduce heat; simmer, covered, about 10 minutes or until potato is tender.
3 Add fish; simmer, uncovered, about 4 minutes or until fish is barely cooked. Serve soup sprinkled with chives. Accompany with fresh, crusty white bread, if you like.

prep + cook time *45 minutes* **serves** *4*
nutritional count per serving *19.5g total fat (11.6g saturated fat); 1810kJ (433 cal); 28.4g carbohydrate; 34.8g protein; 2.4g fibre*

Use any extra finely chopped vegetables as a filling for baked capsicums, zucchini or mushrooms.

minestrone

1 cup (200g) dried borlotti beans
1 tablespoon olive oil
1 medium brown onion (150g),
    chopped coarsely
1 clove garlic, crushed
¼ cup (70g) tomato paste
1.5 litres (6 cups) water
2 cups (500ml) vegetable stock
700g bottled tomato pasta sauce
1 trimmed celery stalk (100g), chopped finely
1 medium carrot (120g), chopped finely
1 medium zucchini (120g), chopped finely
80g green beans, trimmed, chopped finely
¾ cup (135g) macaroni
⅓ cup coarsely chopped fresh basil

1 Place borlotti beans in medium bowl, cover with water; stand overnight, drain. Rinse under cold water; drain.
2 Heat oil in large saucepan; cook onion and garlic, stirring, until onion softens. Add paste; cook, stirring, 2 minutes. Add borlotti beans, the water, stock and pasta sauce; bring to the boil. Reduce heat; simmer, uncovered, about 1 hour or until beans are tender.
3 Add celery to soup; simmer, uncovered, 10 minutes. Add carrot, zucchini and green beans; simmer, uncovered, about 20 minutes or until carrot is tender. Add pasta; simmer until pasta is tender.
4 Serve bowls of soup sprinkled with basil.
prep + cook time *2 hours 30 minutes (+ standing)*
serves *6*
nutritional count per serving *5.5g total fat (1g saturated fat); 1095kJ (262 cal); 39.9g carbohydrate; 9.4g protein; 6.5g fibre*

Compare the weight and price of all food items before you make your selection.

lentil & garlic soup
with yogurt

1 tablespoon olive oil
10 cloves garlic, sliced thinly
2 sprigs fresh thyme
2 cups (400g) australian fine green lentils
2 cups (500ml) vegetable stock
2 litres (8 cups) water
175g watercress, trimmed, chopped coarsely

minted yogurt
1 cup (280g) yogurt
1 tablespoon lemon juice
¼ cup coarsely chopped fresh mint

1 Heat oil in large saucepan; cook garlic and thyme, stirring, until garlic softens. Stir in lentils then stock and the water; bring to the boil. Reduce heat; simmer, covered, about 35 minutes or until lentils soften.
2 Meanwhile, make minted yogurt.
3 Blend or process soup, in batches, until pureed; return to pan. Add watercress to soup; cook, stirring, until wilted. Serve soup with minted yogurt.
minted yogurt Combine ingredients in medium bowl.
prep + cook time *55 minutes* **serves** *6*
nutritional count per serving *6.5g total fat (1.9g saturated fat); 1158kJ (277 cal); 28.9g carbohydrate; 20.1g protein; 16.7g fibre*

If cheaper, buy canned whole tomatoes as opposed to canned crushed or diced tomatoes. You can easily cut them up in a bowl.

white bean & chickpea soup with risoni

1 tablespoon olive oil
1 medium brown onion (150g), chopped coarsely
1 large carrot (180g), chopped coarsely
2 cloves garlic, sliced thinly
2 tablespoons tomato paste
2 teaspoons ground cumin
2 x 400g cans crushed tomatoes
1 litre (4 cups) vegetable stock
400g can chickpeas, rinsed, drained
400g can white beans, rinsed, drained
⅓ cup (75g) risoni

1 Heat oil in large saucepan; cook onion and carrot, stirring, until carrot softens. Add garlic, paste and cumin; cook, stirring, until garlic softens.
2 Add undrained tomatoes and stock to pan; bring to the boil. Add chickpeas and beans; return to the boil. Add risoni; boil about 10 minutes or until risoni is tender.
prep + cook time *45 minutes* **serves 4**
nutritional count per serving *7.8g total fat (1.4g saturated fat); 1359kJ (325 cal); 41.9g carbohydrate; 15.5g protein; 11.6g fibre*

black-eyed bean & ham soup

1 cup (200g) black-eyed beans
1 tablespoon olive oil
1 trimmed celery stalk (100g), chopped coarsely
1 small brown onion (80g), chopped coarsely
1 medium carrot (120g), chopped coarsely
1 bay leaf
2 cloves garlic
1.2kg ham hock
1 litre (4 cups) chicken stock
2 litres (8 cups) water
125g trimmed silver beet, shredded finely
2 tablespoons cider vinegar

1 Place beans in medium bowl, cover with water; stand overnight, rinse, drain.
2 Heat oil in large saucepan, add celery, onion and carrot; cook until vegetables are soft. Add bay leaf, garlic, ham hock, stock and the water; bring to the boil. Reduce heat; simmer, uncovered, 1 hour.
3 Add beans to soup; simmer, uncovered, about 1 hour or until beans are tender.
4 Remove hock from soup. When cool enough to handle, remove meat from hock. Discard bone; shred meat coarsely, return to soup.
5 Add silver beet to soup; cook, stirring, until wilted. Remove from heat; stir in vinegar.

prep + cook time *2 hours 55 minutes (+ standing)*
serves *6*
nutritional count per serving *7.2g total fat (1.8g saturated fat); 945kJ (226 cal); 16.1g carbohydrate; 21.2g protein; 6.3g fibre*

You need approximately
500g of untrimmed
silver beet for this recipe.

french onion soup with gruyère croûtons

50g butter
4 large brown onions (800g), sliced thinly
¾ cup (180ml) dry white wine
3 cups (750ml) water
1 litre (4 cups) beef stock
1 bay leaf
1 tablespoon plain flour
1 teaspoon fresh thyme leaves

gruyère croûtons
1 small french bread (150g), cut in 1.5cm slices
½ cup (60g) coarsely grated gruyère cheese

1 Melt butter in large saucepan, add onion; cook, stirring occasionally, about 30 minutes or until caramelised.
2 Meanwhile, bring wine to the boil in large saucepan; boil 1 minute then stir in the water, stock and bay leaf; return to the boil. Remove from heat.
3 Stir flour into onion mixture; cook, stirring, 2 minutes. Gradually add hot broth mixture to onion mixture, stirring, until mixture boils and thickens slightly. Reduce heat; simmer, uncovered, stirring occasionally, 20 minutes. Discard bay leaf; stir in thyme.
4 Meanwhile, make gruyère croûtons.
5 Serve bowls of soup topped with croûtons. Sprinkle with extra fresh thyme leaves, if you like.
gruyère croûtons Preheat grill. Toast bread on one side then turn and sprinkle with cheese; grill croûtons until cheese browns lightly.
prep + cook time *1 hour 10 minutes* **serves 4**
nutritional count per serving *16.7g total fat (10g saturated fat); 1522kJ (364 cal); 31.1g carbohydrate; 13.4g protein; 3.9g fibre*

Use freshly ground pepper as opposed to ready-ground pepper. Invest in a strong, quality pepper mill and buy black and white peppercorns in sealed packets to ensure freshness.

pea & ham soup

1 medium brown onion (150g), chopped coarsely
2 trimmed celery stalks (200g), chopped coarsely
2 bay leaves
1.5kg ham hocks
2.5 litres (10 cups) water
1 teaspoon cracked black pepper
2 cups (375g) split green peas

1 Combine onion, celery, bay leaves, hocks, the water and pepper in large saucepan; bring to the boil. Reduce heat; simmer, covered, about 1½ hours. Add peas; simmer, covered, 30 minutes or until peas are tender.
2 Remove ham hocks; when cool enough to handle, remove meat from hocks. Shred meat finely. Discard bones, fat and skin; remove and discard bay leaves.
3 Blend or process half the soup mixture, in batches, until smooth; return to pan with remaining soup mixture and ham. Reheat soup.
prep + cook time *2 hours 15 minutes*   serves *6*
nutritional count per serving   *4.9g total fat (1.4g saturated fat); 1162kJ (278 cal); 31g carbohydrate; 23.5g protein; 7.3g fibre*

Use lamb shanks that have not been french-trimmed or 2kg lamb neck chops in this soup. The money saved will more than make up for any extra effort expended trimming excess fat from the meat before cooking or skimming fat off the soup's surface.

lamb & barley soup

You need approximately 1kg of untrimmed silver beet for this recipe.

1.5kg french-trimmed lamb shanks
3 litres (12 cups) water
¾ cup (150g) pearl barley
1 medium carrot (120g), sliced thinly
1 medium leek (350g), sliced thinly
2 trimmed celery stalks (200g), sliced thinly
1 tablespoon curry powder
250g trimmed silver beet, chopped coarsely

1 Combine lamb, the water and barley in large saucepan; bring to the boil. Reduce heat; simmer, uncovered, 1 hour, skimming surface and stirring occasionally. Add carrot, leek and celery; simmer, uncovered, 10 minutes.
2 Remove lamb from soup mixture. When cool enough to handle, remove meat; chop coarsely. Discard bones and any fat or skin.
3 Dry-fry curry powder in small saucepan until fragrant. Return meat to soup with curry powder and silver beet; cook, uncovered, until silver beet wilts.
prep + cook time *1 hour 40 minutes* serves *6*
nutritional count per serving *13.3g total fat (5.7g saturated fat); 1404kJ (336 cal); 18.9g carbohydrate; 31.8g protein; 6.4g fibre*

chunky beef & vegetable soup

2 tablespoons olive oil
600g gravy beef, trimmed, cut into 2cm pieces
1 medium brown onion (150g), chopped coarsely
1 clove garlic, crushed
1.5 litres (6 cups) water
1 cup (250ml) beef stock
400g can diced tomatoes
2 trimmed celery stalks (200g), cut into 1cm pieces
1 medium carrot (120g), cut into 1cm pieces
2 small potatoes (240g), cut into 1cm pieces
310g can corn kernels, rinsed, drained
½ cup (60g) frozen peas

1 Heat half of the oil in large saucepan; cook beef, in batches, until browned.
2 Heat remaining oil in same pan; cook onion and garlic, stirring, until onion softens. Return beef to pan with the water, stock and undrained tomatoes; bring to the boil. Reduce heat; simmer, covered, 1½ hours.
3 Add celery, carrot and potato to soup; simmer, uncovered, about 20 minutes or until vegetables are tender.
4 Add corn and peas to soup; stir over heat until peas are tender.

prep + cook time *2 hours 20 minutes*   serves *4*
nutritional count per serving *17g total fat (4.3g saturated fat); 1768kJ (423 cal); 26.7g carbohydrate; 36.9g protein; 7.5g fibre*

lamb shank & vegetable soup

4 lamb shanks (1kg)
2 medium carrots (240g), chopped coarsely
2 medium white onions (300g), chopped coarsely
2 cloves garlic, crushed
2 medium potatoes (400g), chopped coarsely
2 trimmed celery stalks (200g), chopped coarsely
400g can chopped tomatoes
1.5 litres (6 cups) beef or chicken stock
½ cup (125ml) tomato paste
2 medium zucchini (240g), chopped coarsely

1 Place shanks, carrot, onion, garlic, potato, celery, undrained tomatoes, stock and paste in large saucepan; bring to the boil. Reduce heat; simmer, covered, 1 hour.
2 Add zucchini to soup, simmer, uncovered, further 30 minutes or until shanks are tender.
3 Remove shanks from soup. When cool enough to handle, remove meat from bones, discard bones. Return meat to soup, stir until heated through.
prep + cook time *2 hours* **serves** *4*
nutritional count per serving *9.2g total fat (3.9g saturated fat); 1513kJ (362 cal); 29.2g carbohydrate; 39.7g protein; 8.5g fibre*

snacks

ham, egg & cheese toastie

2 slices wholemeal bread (90g)
1 tablespoon barbecue sauce
30g shaved ham
1 hard-boiled egg, sliced
¼ cup (30g) coarsely grated reduced-fat
   cheddar cheese

1 Spread bread with sauce; top one bread slice with ham, egg and cheese then remaining bread slice.
2 Toast in sandwich press until golden brown.

prep + cook time *10 minutes*   **makes** *1*
nutritional count per toastie *16.1g total fat (6.9g saturated fat); 1898kJ (454 cal); 44.3g carbohydrate; 29.7g protein; 5.9g fibre*

Use leftover bread to make breadcrumbs.
They are tastier and have no additives like
those you buy in a packet. Crumb in a blender
or food processor and freeze in plastic bags.

curried egg sandwiches

6 hard-boiled eggs, chopped coarsely
⅓ cup (100g) mayonnaise
2 teaspoons curry powder
8 slices white bread (360g)
2 cups shredded iceberg lettuce

1 Use a fork to mash egg, mayonnaise and curry
powder in a medium bowl.
2 Top half the bread with egg mixture then lettuce;
top with remaining bread. Remove crusts. Cut into
triangles to serve.
prep time *15 minutes*   **makes 4**
nutritional count per sandwich *18.4g total fat
(3.9g saturated fat); 1793kJ (429 cal); 45.9g
carbohydrate; 18.1g protein; 3.4g fibre*

Synonymous with French cuisine, croque monsieur, and his sister, croque madame, are that nation's answer to a toasted sandwich.

croque monsieur

8 slices wholemeal bread (360g)
8 slices leg ham (180g)
40g butter

cheese sauce
20g butter
1 tablespoon plain flour
¾ cup (180ml) milk
¾ cup (90g) coarsely grated cheddar cheese
1 tablespoon finely chopped fresh flat-leaf parsley

1 Make cheese sauce.
2 Spread sauce over bread slices; top four slices with ham then top with remaining bread.
3 Melt butter in large frying pan. Add sandwiches; cook, in batches, until browned both sides.
cheese sauce Melt butter in small saucepan, add flour; cook, stirring, until mixture bubbles and thickens. Gradually add milk; cook, stirring, until sauce boils and thickens. Remove from heat; stir in cheese and parsley.
prep + cook time *30 minutes* **makes** *4*
nutritional count per sandwich *25.9g total fat (15g saturated fat); 2077kJ (497 cal); 38.4g carbohydrate; 24.8g protein; 5.8g fibre*

When it comes to breakfast options such as rolled oats or cereals, buy them in large packets or boxes instead of the individual portions that are also available. They are comparatively cheaper.

baked beans, bacon, tomato & chives

2 medium tomatoes (300g), chopped coarsely
1 tablespoon finely chopped chives
420g can baked beans in tomato sauce
4 rindless bacon rashers (260g), chopped coarsely
½ large loaf turkish bread (215g), halved

1 Preheat grill.
2 Combine tomato and chives in small bowl.
3 Heat beans in small saucepan.
4 Meanwhile, cook bacon, stirring, in heated small frying pan until crisp; drain on absorbent paper.
5 Cut bread pieces horizontally; toast cut sides. Top toast with beans, bacon and tomato mixture; grill about 2 minutes or until hot.

prep + cook time *10 minutes*   **serves** *4*
nutiritional count per serving *10.4g total fat (3.2g saturated fat); 1450kJ (347 cal); 34.5g carbohydrate; 22g protein; 7.4g fibre*

The tuna filling can be refrigerated for up to 2 days before assembling the baguette.

mediterranean tuna baguette

1 medium potato (200g), diced
2 tablespoons olive oil
1 tablespoon red wine vinegar
1 teaspoon dijon mustard
1 tablespoon finely chopped black olives
1 medium tomato (150g), seeded, chopped finely
185g can tuna in springwater, drained
2 small french sticks (300g)
30g mesclun
2 hard-boiled eggs, sliced

1 Cook potato until tender; drain.
2 Meanwhile, place oil, vinegar and mustard in screw-top jar; shake well.
3 Combine potato and dressing in medium bowl with olives, tomato and tuna.
4 Halve bread sticks crossways then split in half. Sandwich mesclun, egg and tuna mixture between bread pieces.

prep + cook time *30 minutes* makes *4*
nutritional count per baguette *15.7g total fat (2.9g saturated fat); 1781kJ (426 cal); 47.9g carbohydrate; 20.9g protein; 4.2g fibre*

Chunks of leftover ham are good to use in omelettes and creamy sauces for pasta.

croque madame

8 slices wholemeal bread (360g)
8 slices leg ham (180g)
40g butter
4 eggs

cheese sauce
20g butter
1 tablespoon plain flour
¾ cup (180ml) milk
½ cup (60g) finely grated cheddar cheese
1 tablespoon finely chopped fresh
    flat-leaf parsley

1 Make cheese sauce.
2 Spread sauce onto bread slices. Top four slices with ham then remaining bread.
3 Melt butter in large frying pan. Add sandwiches; toast, in batches, until browned both sides.
4 Fry eggs in same pan until cooked. Top each sandwich with an egg.
cheese sauce Melt butter in small saucepan, add flour; cook, stirring, until mixture bubbles and thickens. Gradually add milk; cook, stirring, until sauce boils and thickens. Remove from heat; stir in cheese and parsley.
prep + cook time *35 minutes* makes *4*
nutritional count per sandwich *28.6g total fat (15g saturated fat); 2261kJ (541 cal); 38.6g carbohydrate; 29.5g protein; 8.3g fibre*

spinach, ham & poached egg

4 eggs
½ large loaf turkish bread (215g), halved
75g baby spinach leaves
150g shaved ham

1 Half-fill large frying pan with water; bring to the boil. Break one egg into a cup then slide into pan; repeat with remaining eggs. When all eggs are in pan, allow water to return to the boil. Cover pan, turn off heat; stand about 4 minutes or until a light film of egg white sets over yolks. Remove eggs, one at a time, using slotted spoon; place spoon on absorbent-paper-lined saucer to blot up poaching liquid.
2 Meanwhile, cut bread pieces horizontally; toast cut sides. Top toast with spinach, ham and eggs.
prep + cook time *10 minutes*   serves *4*
nutritional count per serving *8.4g total fat (2.4g saturated fat); 1062kJ (254 cal); 24.3g carbohydrate; 18.9g protein; 1.9g fibre*

ham & cheese
pinwheels

6 eggs, beaten lightly
2 cups (300g) self-raising flour
1 tablespoon caster sugar
30g butter
¾ cup (180ml) low-fat milk
¼ cup (70g) tomato paste
175g shaved ham, cut into thin strips
1 cup (120g) coarsely grated reduced-fat
   cheddar cheese

1 Preheat oven to 200°C/180°C fan-forced. Oil 19cm x 29cm slice pan.
2 Cook egg in oiled medium frying pan over low heat, stirring constantly, until scrambled.
3 Sift flour and sugar into medium bowl; rub in butter. Stir in milk; mix to a soft, sticky dough. Knead dough on floured surface; roll dough to 30cm x 40cm shape.
4 Spread tomato paste over dough; sprinkle with ham, top with egg then sprinkle with cheese.
5 Starting from long side, roll dough firmly; trim ends. Cut roll into 12 slices; place pinwheels, cut-side up, in single layer, in pan. Bake about 30 minutes. Serve pinwheels warm.

prep + cook time **1 hour**   makes **12**
nutritional count per pinwheel **7.5g total fat (3.9g saturated fat); 865kJ (207 cal); 20.8g carbohydrate; 12.3g protein; 1.2g fibre**

Buy fruit and vegetables when they are in season – they're at their cheapest and their best.

bean nachos

2 x 420g cans kidney beans, rinsed, drained
⅓ cup (85g) chunky tomato salsa
⅓ cup finely chopped fresh coriander
230g bag corn chips
1½ cups (180g) coarsely grated cheddar cheese
2 cups (120g) finely shredded iceberg lettuce
1 small tomato (90g), chopped coarsely
½ small avocado (100g), chopped coarsely
2 tablespoons lime juice

1 Preheat oven to 220°C/200°C fan-forced.
2 Combine half the beans with salsa; mash until chunky. Stir in remaining beans and coriander.
3 Spread half the chips in medium shallow baking dish; top with half the cheese and half the bean mixture. Top with remaining chips, remaining cheese then remaining bean mixture. Cook 10 minutes.
4 Toss lettuce, tomato and avocado in medium bowl with juice. Serve nachos topped with salad.
prep + cook time *20 minutes*   serves *6*
nutritional count per serving *24.5g total fat (11.6g saturated fat); 1856kJ (444 cal); 33.7g carbohydrate; 17.3g protein; 10.8g fibre*

We used rindless shortcut bacon here, but you can use trimmed bacon rashers if you prefer.

BLT on croissant

12 slices rindless shortcut bacon (420g)
4 large croissants (320g)
2 small tomatoes (180g), sliced thinly
8 large butter lettuce leaves

aïoli
½ cup (150g) mayonnaise
1 clove garlic, crushed
1 tablespoon finely chopped fresh flat-leaf parsley

1 Preheat grill.
2 Cook bacon in large frying pan until crisp.
3 Meanwhile, make aïoli.
4 Toast croissants under grill about 30 seconds. Split croissants in half; spread aïoli over one half of each croissant then top with bacon, tomato, lettuce and remaining croissant half.
aïoli Combine ingredients in small bowl.

prep + cook time *15 minutes* serves *4*
nutritional count per serving *36.8g total fat (13.9g saturated fat); 2592kJ (620 cal); 39.5g carbohydrate; 31.4g protein; 3.8g fibre*

avocado, bacon
& tomato panini

8 rindless bacon rashers (520g)
4 panini bread rolls
⅓ cup (100g) mayonnaise
1 medium avocado (250g), sliced thinly
2 medium tomatoes (300g), sliced thinly
60g mesclun

1 Preheat grill.
2 Cook bacon in heated medium frying pan until crisp.
3 Meanwhile, split panini; toast cut sides under grill.
4 Spread panini with mayonnaise; fill with avocado, tomato, mesclun and bacon.

prep + cook time *15 minutes* makes *4*
nutritional count per panini *25.8g total fat
(6.4g saturated fat); 1731kJ (414 cal); 24g
carbohydrate; 20.3g protein; 3.1g fibre*

Use turkish rolls if panini
rolls aren't available.

beans on toast

2 cups (400g) dried cannellini beans
1 tablespoon olive oil
1 large brown onion (200g), chopped coarsely
2 cloves garlic, sliced thinly
2 rindless bacon rashers (130g), chopped coarsely
2 tablespoons brown sugar
¼ cup (60ml) maple syrup
1 tablespoon dijon mustard
400g can chopped tomatoes
1 litre (4 cups) water
6 x 1cm-thick slices sourdough bread
2 tablespoons coarsely chopped fresh
　　flat-leaf parsley

1 Place beans in large bowl, cover with water; stand overnight, drain. Rinse under cold water, drain.
2 Heat oil in large saucepan, add onion, garlic and bacon; cook, stirring, until onion softens. Stir in beans, sugar, syrup and mustard. Add undrained tomatoes and the water; bring to the boil. Reduce heat; simmer, covered, about 2 hours or until beans are tender.
3 Uncover; cook, stirring occasionally, about 30 minutes or until mixture thickens. Serve beans on toasted sourdough bread; sprinkle with parsley.
prep + cook time *2 hours 55 minutes (+ standing)*
serves *6*
nutritional count per serving *6.3g total fat (1.1g saturated fat); 1626kJ (389 cal); 53.1g carbohydrate; 22.2g protein; 14.5g fibre*

egg dishes

huevos rancheros

6 x 15cm corn tortillas
125g can kidney beans, rinsed, drained
½ cup (130g) bottled chunky tomato salsa
1 small tomato (90g), chopped coarsely
2 tablespoons coarsely chopped fresh coriander
6 eggs
½ cup (60g) coarsely grated cheddar cheese
1 small avocado (200g), chopped coarsely
1 tablespoon lime juice

1 Preheat oven to 200°C/180°C fan-forced. Grease six-hole (¾-cup/180ml) texas muffin pan.
2 Soften tortillas according to manufacturer's instructions. Gently press one tortilla into each pan hole to form a cup.
3 Combine beans, salsa, tomato and coriander in small bowl; divide half the bean mixture among tortilla cups. Break one egg into each cup. Sprinkle with cheese.
4 Bake about 12 minutes or until eggs are cooked.
5 Meanwhile, stir avocado and juice into remaining bean mixture.
6 Serve huevos rancheros topped with avocado mixture and, if you like, accompanied by sour cream and lime wedges.

prep + cook time *25 minutes* **makes** *6*
nutritional count per huevos rancheros
14.5g total fat (5g saturated fat); 961kJ (230 cal); 11.8g carbohydrate; 12.1g protein; 2.8g fibre

tortilla de patata

20g butter
¼ cup (60ml) olive oil
3 medium potatoes (600g), chopped finely
1 medium brown onion (150g), chopped finely
8 eggs
½ teaspoon chilli powder

1 Preheat oven to 180°C/160°C fan-forced.
2 Melt butter with oil in 22cm-base ovenproof frying pan; cook potato and onion, stirring occasionally, until potato is tender.
3 Meanwhile, whisk eggs and chilli powder in medium jug.
4 Add egg mixture to pan. Cook, uncovered, over low heat, about 5 minutes or until just set.
5 Place pan in oven; cook, uncovered, about 10 minutes or until browned lightly. Carefully turn tortilla onto plate. Cut into wedges; serve with a side salad.

prep + cook time *35 minutes*   serves *4*
nutritional count per serving *28.4g total fat (7.8g saturated fat); 1747kJ (418 cal); 22g carbohydrate; 17.5g protein; 28.4g fibre*

Buy ingredients for two meals. Freeze one portion to eat at a later date.

kumara bacon & egg bake

1 large kumara (500g), sliced thinly
1½ teaspoons ground cumin
5 rindless bacon rashers (325g), chopped finely
1 medium brown onion (150g), chopped finely
8 eggs
¼ cup (60ml) cream
1 cup (120g) coarsely grated cheddar cheese

1 Preheat oven to 180°C/160°C fan-forced. Oil 2.5 litre (10-cup) baking dish.
2 Boil, steam or microwave kumara 5 minutes. Drain; pat dry with absorbent paper. Place in single layer over base of dish; sprinkle with ½ teaspoon of the cumin.
3 Meanwhile, cook bacon and onion over heat in medium frying pan about 5 minutes or until onion softens. Stir in remaining cumin, spread mixture over kumara.
4 Whisk eggs, cream and cheese in medium bowl; pour over kumara mixture. Bake, uncovered, in oven, 30 minutes.

prep + cook time *55 minutes*   **serves** *4*
nutritional count per serving *31.7g total fat (15.6g saturated fat); 2195kJ (525 cal); 18.1g carbohydrate; 41.1g protein; 2.4g fibre*

fish & potato soufflés

300g potatoes, chopped coarsely
300g fish fillets
2 tablespoons packaged breadcrumbs
50g butter
1 small brown onion (80g), chopped finely
2 tablespoons plain flour
¾ cup (180ml) milk
2 egg yolks
¼ cup (20g) finely grated parmesan cheese
2 tablespoons finely chopped garlic chives
1 teaspoon finely grated lemon rind
3 eggs whites

1 Boil, steam or microwave potato until tender; drain. Mash until smooth.
2 Meanwhile, cook fish in medium saucepan of simmering water, uncovered, about 4 minutes or until cooked. When cool enough to handle, flake fish.
3 Preheat oven to 220°C/200°C fan-forced. Oil six-hole (¾-cup/180ml) texas muffin pan.
4 Divide breadcrumbs among pan holes; shake pan to coat bases and sides with breadcrumbs. Place pan on oven tray.
5 Melt butter in medium saucepan; cook onion, stirring, until onion softens. Add flour; cook, stirring, until mixture thickens and bubbles. Gradually stir in milk; cook, stirring, until mixture boils and thickens. Transfer mixture to large bowl; stir in egg yolks, cheese, chives, rind, potato and fish.
6 Beat egg whites in small bowl with electric mixer until soft peaks form. Fold egg whites into fish mixture, in two batches. Divide soufflé mixture among pan holes. Bake about 20 minutes.
7 Gently turn soufflés out; serve immediately, top-side up with, if you like, sour cream and lemon wedges.
prep + cook time *45 minutes* **makes** *6*
nutritional count per soufflé *14.7g total fat (7.4g saturated fat); 1045kJ (250 cal); 12.2g carbohydrate; 16.9g protein; 1.1g fibre*

tomato, basil & bacon omelette

1 tablespoon olive oil
1 small red onion (100g), sliced thinly
1 clove garlic, crushed
4 rindless bacon rashers (260g), chopped coarsely
1 small tomato (90g), sliced thinly
8 eggs, beaten lightly
1 cup (100g) packaged breadcrumbs
⅓ cup finely chopped fresh basil
½ cup loosely packed fresh basil leaves
1 teaspoon balsamic vinegar

1 Preheat grill.
2 Heat half the oil in medium frying pan; cook onion, garlic and bacon, stirring, until onion softens. Arrange tomato slices over bacon mixture.
3 Carefully pour combined egg, breadcrumbs and chopped basil into pan; cook, over low heat, until omelette is almost set.
4 Place pan under grill until omelette sets and top is browned lightly.
5 Carefully turn omelette, bottom-side up, onto serving plate, sprinkle with basil leaves; drizzle with combined remaining oil and vinegar.

prep + cook time *35 minutes*   **serves** *4*
nutritional count per serving *16.9g total fat (4.4g saturated fat); 1300kJ (311 cal); 18.7g carbohydrate; 20.2g protein; 2g fibre*

You need a medium frying pan with a heatproof handle and a 20cm base for this recipe. If the pan handle is not heatproof, wrap it tightly in a few layers of foil; place the pan under the grill, but keep the handle away from the heat, if possible.

herb omelette with sauteed mushrooms

2 tablespoons finely chopped fresh flat-leaf parsley
2 tablespoons finely chopped fresh chervil
2 tablespoons finely chopped fresh chives
2 tablespoons finely chopped fresh tarragon
50g butter
2 tablespoons olive oil
250g swiss brown mushrooms, halved
½ cup (125ml) water
2 teaspoons finely grated lemon rind
1 tablespoon lemon juice
12 eggs

1 Combine herbs in small bowl.
2 Heat 30g of the butter and 1 tablespoon of the oil in large deep frying pan. Add mushrooms; cook, stirring, 5 minutes. Stir in 2 tablespoons of the water; cook, stirring, until water evaporates and mushrooms are tender. Remove from heat; stir in rind, juice and 2 tablespoons of the herb mixture. Cover to keep warm.
3 Gently whisk eggs and remaining water in a large bowl, whisk in remaining herb mixture.
4 Heat a quarter of the remaining butter and 1 teaspoon of the remaining oil in medium frying pan. When butter mixture bubbles, pour a quarter of the egg mixture into pan; cook over medium heat, tilting pan, until egg is almost set. Tilt pan backwards; fold omelette in half. Cook 30 seconds then slide onto serving plate.
5 Repeat process with remaining butter, oil and egg mixture, wiping out pan before each addition to make a total of 4 omelettes. Serve omelettes topped with sautéed mushrooms.

prep + cook time *30 minutes* serves *4*
nutritional count per serving *35.3g total fat (12.9g saturated fat); 1714kJ (410 cal); 1g carbohydrate; 22.4g protein; 1.8g fibre*

Learn the cost of grocery items you buy frequently, then you'll know a genuine sale price when it is advertised.

roast kumara & spinach frittata

2 medium kumara (800g)
1 tablespoon olive oil
2 teaspoons ground cumin
50g baby spinach leaves, chopped coarsely
¼ cup (20g) finely grated parmesan cheese
6 eggs, beaten lightly
⅔ cup (160ml) cream

1 Preheat oven to 180°C/160°C fan-forced. Grease six-hole (¾-cup/180ml) texas muffin pan; line bases with baking paper.
2 Peel kumara; cut into 5mm slices. Combine kumara, oil and cumin in large, shallow baking dish; roast about 20 minutes or until tender. Cool 10 minutes.
3 Divide spinach, cheese then kumara among pan holes, finishing with kumara.
4 Whisk egg and cream in medium bowl; pour into pan holes.
5 Bake about 25 minutes. Stand in pan 5 minutes; using palette knife, loosen frittata from edge of pan before turning out, top-side up.
prep + cook time *1 hour*   **makes** *6*
nutritional count per frittata *21g total fat (10.3g saturated fat); 1267kJ (303 cal); 16.9g carbohydrate; 10.8g protein; 2.3g fibre*

cooked english
breakfast

50g butter
300g button mushrooms, halved
8 chipolata sausages (240g)
4 rindless bacon rashers (260g)
2 medium tomatoes (300g), halved
1 tablespoon vegetable oil
8 eggs

1 Melt butter in medium saucepan; cook mushrooms, stirring, about 5 minutes or until tender.
2 Cook sausages and bacon in heated oiled large frying pan. Remove from pan; cover to keep warm. Drain fat from pan.
3 Preheat grill. Place tomatoes, cut-side up, onto oven tray, grill until browned lightly.
4 Meanwhile, heat oil in same large frying pan, add eggs; cook eggs until cooked as desired.
5 Serve mushrooms, sausages, bacon, tomato and eggs with toast, if you like.

prep + cook time *20 minutes* **serves** *4*
nutritional count per serving *47.7g total fat (20.2g saturated fat); 2424kJ (580 cal); 3.5g carbohydrate; 34.5g protein; 2.4g fibre*

pasta & pizza

orecchiette boscaiola

375g orecchiette pasta
60g butter
135g pancetta, chopped finely
150g mushrooms, sliced thinly
1 clove garlic, crushed
1 teaspoon cracked black pepper
300ml cream
½ cup (40g) finely grated parmesan cheese

1 Cook pasta in large saucepan of boiling water, uncovered, until just tender; drain.
2 Melt butter in medium frying pan; cook pancetta, stirring, 5 minutes. Add mushrooms and garlic; cook, stirring, 3 minutes.
3 Add pepper and cream; simmer, uncovered, about 5 minutes or until sauce reduces by half.
4 Add cheese; stir over low heat, 2 minutes or until cheese melts. Combine pasta and sauce in large bowl.

prep + cook time *20 minutes* **serves** *4*
nutritional count per serving *53.5g total fat (33.4g saturated fat); 3540kJ (847 cal); 66.6g carbohydrate; 23.6g protein; 4.3g fibre*

A teaspoon of dried chilli flakes cooked with the garlic makes a deliciously hot alternative. If you have some, stir in ¼ cup coarsely chopped fresh flat-leaf parsley or a handful of baby rocket leaves before serving.

pasta with capers & anchovies

375g spaghetti
2 tablespoons olive oil
3 cloves garlic, sliced thinly
¼ cup (50g) drained baby capers, rinsed
10 anchovy fillets, chopped finely
1 tablespoon finely grated lemon rind
1 tablespoon lemon juice

1 Cook pasta in large saucepan of boiling water until tender; drain.
2 Meanwhile, heat oil in medium frying pan; cook garlic, stirring, until fragrant. Add capers and anchovies; stir gently until hot. Pour garlic mixture over pasta; stir in rind and juice.

prep + cook time *15 minutes* serves *4*
nutritional count per serving *11.1g total fat (1.7g saturated fat); 1781kJ (426 cal); 65.6g carbohydrate; 13.3g protein; 3.8g fibre*

Fetta cheese can be used in place of the ricotta cheese. If you have some, stir ⅓ cup loosely packed fresh mint leaves into this recipe.

lemon, pea & ricotta pasta

375g angel hair pasta
2 cups (240g) frozen peas
2 tablespoons olive oil
2 cloves garlic, sliced thinly
2 teaspoons finely grated lemon rind
½ cup (125ml) lemon juice
¾ cup (180g) ricotta cheese, crumbled

1 Cook pasta in large saucepan of boiling water until tender; add peas during last minute of pasta cooking time. Drain, reserving ¼ cup cooking liquid. Rinse pasta and peas under cold water; drain.
2 Meanwhile, heat oil in small frying pan; cook garlic, stirring, until fragrant.
3 Combine pasta and peas in large bowl with reserved cooking liquid, garlic mixture, rind and juice; stir in cheese.

prep + cook time *15 minutes*   serves *4*
nutritional count per serving *15.6g total fat (4.7g saturated fat); 2123kJ (508 cal); 69g carbohydrate; 19g protein; 6.9g fibre*

Add diced leftover chicken or turkey to a white sauce. Season, heat and pour over your favourite pasta or sprinkle with breadcrumbs and cheese and heat in the oven.

spaghetti with pesto

2 cloves garlic, chopped coarsely
⅓ cup (50g) roasted pine nuts
½ cup (40g) finely grated parmesan cheese
2 cups firmly packed fresh basil leaves
½ cup (125ml) olive oil
500g spaghetti
½ cup (40g) flaked parmesan cheese

1 Blend or process garlic, nuts, grated cheese and basil until almost smooth. Gradually add oil in a thin, steady stream, processing until thick.
2 Cook pasta in large saucepan of boiling water, until just tender; drain, reserve ¼ cup of the cooking liquid.
3 Combine pasta, pesto and reserved cooking liquid in large bowl. Serve with flaked cheese.
prep + cook time *25 minutes* serves *4*
nutritional count per serving *45.2g total fat (8.9g saturated fat); 3578kJ (859 cal); 86.2g carbohydrate; 23.6g protein; 5.6g fibre*

If a recipe calls for an expensive ingredient such as crab meat, you can use tuna instead.

tuna & chilli pasta

Baby capers can be added to this recipe. Stir in ⅓ cup coarsely chopped fresh basil leaves just before serving, if you like.

375g angel hair pasta
425g can tuna in oil
4 cloves garlic, sliced thinly
1 teaspoon dried chilli flakes
⅓ cup (80ml) dry white wine
400g can chopped tomatoes
1 tablespoon lemon juice

1 Cook pasta in large saucepan of boiling water until tender; drain, reserving ¼ cup cooking liquid. Rinse pasta under cold water, drain.
2 Meanwhile, drain tuna, reserving 2 tablespoons of the oil. Heat oil in medium frying pan, add garlic; cook, stirring, until fragrant. Add chilli and wine; cook, uncovered, until wine is almost evaporated. Add undrained tomatoes, tuna and reserved cooking liquid; simmer until liquid has reduced slightly. Remove from heat; stir in juice.
3 Combine pasta and sauce in large bowl.
prep + cook time *15 minutes*   serves *4*
nutritional count per serving *22.3g total fat (3.2g saturated fat); 2617kJ (626 cal); 67.5g carbohydrate; 32.5g protein; 4.8g fibre*

Select your supermarket carefully. Make your decision based on quality and freshness of the meat, fruit and vegetables as well as price.

pumpkin & goats cheese lasagne

700g piece butternut pumpkin, peeled
1 tablespoon olive oil
3 fresh lasagne sheets (150g)
150g baby spinach leaves
120g goats cheese, chopped finely
¼ cup (20g) finely grated parmesan cheese

white sauce
20g butter
1 tablespoon plain flour
1½ cups (375ml) milk
¼ cup (20g) finely grated parmesan cheese

1 Preheat oven to 200°C/180°C fan-forced. Grease six-hole (¾-cup/180ml) texas muffin pan; line each pan hole with two criss-crossed 5cm x 20cm strips of baking paper.
2 Cut pumpkin lengthways into 1cm-thick slices. Cut six 7cm rounds and six 8cm rounds from pumpkin slices. Brush pumpkin rounds with oil; place in large baking dish in a single layer. Roast about 15 minutes or until tender.
3 Meanwhile, cut six 7cm rounds and twelve 8cm rounds from lasagne sheets.
4 Make white sauce.

5 Boil, steam or microwave spinach until wilted; drain. Refresh in cold water; drain. Squeeze out excess moisture. Chop spinach coarsely; spread out on absorbent paper.
6 Divide a third of the white sauce among pan holes; place one small pasta round in each hole; top with half the goats cheese, half the spinach then a small pumpkin round. Repeat layers with another third of the sauce, six large pasta rounds and remaining goats cheese, spinach and pumpkin. Top lasagne stacks with remaining pasta rounds and white sauce; sprinkle with parmesan.
7 Bake about 25 minutes or until browned lightly. Stand lasagne in pan 5 minutes. Using baking paper strips as lifters, carefully remove lasagne from pan holes. Serve top-side up.
white sauce Melt butter in medium saucepan, add flour; cook, stirring, 1 minute. Gradually stir in milk; cook, stirring, until sauce boils and thickens. Stir in cheese.

prep + cook time *1 hour 10 minutes*   makes *6*
nutritional count per stack   *14.1g total fat (7.6g saturated fat); 1016kJ (243 cal); 17g carbohydrate; 11.1g protein; 2.3g fibre*

We've used penne pasta in this recipe, but feel free to use spaghetti, if you prefer. Stir in ⅓ cup loosely packed fresh basil leaves just before serving, if you like.

penne bolognese

2 tablespoons olive oil
1 small brown onion (80g), chopped finely
1 medium carrot (120g), chopped finely
1 trimmed celery stalk (100g), chopped finely
2 cloves garlic, sliced thinly
500g beef mince
500g pork mince
½ cup (125ml) milk
½ cup (125ml) dry white wine
2 x 400g cans crushed tomatoes
1 cup (250ml) beef stock
500g penne pasta

1 Heat oil in large saucepan, add onion, carrot, celery and garlic; cook, stirring, until celery softens. Add minces; cook, stirring, until browned. Add milk and wine; simmer, uncovered, until liquid is almost evaporated. Add undrained tomatoes; cook, stirring, 5 minutes. Add stock; bring to the boil. Reduce heat; simmer, covered, 30 minutes.
2 Meanwhile, cook pasta in large saucepan of boiling water until tender; drain. Serve sauce with pasta.
prep + cook time *1 hour 15 minutes* **serves** *6*
nutritional count per serving *19.8g total fat (6.2g saturated fat); 2700kJ (646 cal); 64.4g carbohydrate; 45.7g protein; 5.6g fibre*

Meatballs can be made and fried a day ahead; keep, covered, in the refrigerator until the sauce is made. To save time when making the recipe on another occasion, double the meatball quantities and freeze half of them after frying. Thaw meatballs overnight in refrigerator before adding to the sauce.

spaghetti & meatballs

500g pork mince
2 tablespoons coarsely chopped
   fresh flat-leaf parsley
1 clove garlic, crushed
1 egg
1 cup (70g) stale breadcrumbs
1 tablespoon tomato paste
2 tablespoons olive oil
400g can tomatoes
600ml bottled tomato pasta sauce
375g spaghetti
⅓ cup (25g) finely grated romano cheese

1 Combine pork, parsley, garlic, egg, breadcrumbs and paste in large bowl; roll tablespoons of mixture into balls. Heat oil in large saucepan; cook meatballs, in batches, until browned all over.
2 Place undrained crushed tomatoes and sauce in same pan; bring to the boil. Return meatballs to pan, reduce heat; simmer, uncovered, about 10 minutes or until meatballs are cooked through.
3 Meanwhile, cook pasta in large saucepan of boiling water, uncovered, until just tender; drain. Divide pasta among serving bowls; top with meatballs, sprinkle with cheese.
prep + cook time *35 minutes* **serves 4**
nutritional count per serving *24.2g total fat (6.5g saturated fat); 3269kJ (782 cal); 89.1g carbohydrate; 46.6g protein; 8.7g fibre*

baked penne with
kumara & spinach

2 medium red onions (340g), cut into wedges
2 small kumara (600g), sliced thickly
2 tablespoons olive oil
375g penne pasta
250g frozen spinach, thawed, drained
1½ cups (360g) ricotta cheese
1 clove garlic, crushed
¼ cup (60ml) cream
2 x 400g cans crushed tomatoes
¼ cup (40g) pine nuts
½ cup (40g) finely grated parmesan cheese

1 Preheat oven to 220°C/200°C fan-forced.
2 Combine onion and kumara with oil in large baking dish; roast, uncovered, stirring once, about 40 minutes or until tender.
3 Meanwhile, cook pasta in large saucepan of boiling water until tender; drain.
4 Combine pasta in large bowl with spinach, ricotta, garlic, cream and tomatoes.
5 Spread kumara mixture over base of 3-litre (12-cup) baking dish. Top with pasta mixture; sprinkle with nuts and parmesan. Bake, covered, 10 minutes. Uncover; bake about 5 minutes or until browned lightly.

prep + cook time *1 hour 10 minutes*   serves *6*
nutritional count per serving *25.3g total fat (9.8g saturated fat); 2450kJ (586 cal); 63.4g carbohydrate; 21.9g protein; 8.4g fibre*

macaroni cheese

300g macaroni pasta
4 rindless bacon rashers (260g), chopped finely
50g butter
⅓ cup (50g) plain flour
1 litre (4 cups) milk
1 cup (120g) coarsely grated cheddar cheese
½ cup (40g) finely grated pecorino cheese
2 tablespoons wholegrain mustard
½ cup (35g) stale breadcrumbs
20g butter, extra

1 Preheat oven to 180°C/160°C fan-forced. Oil deep 2-litre (8 cup) ovenproof dish.
2 Cook pasta in large saucepan of boiling water until tender; drain.
3 Meanwhile, cook bacon in medium saucepan, stirring, until crisp; drain on absorbent paper.
4 Melt butter in same pan, add flour; cook, stirring, 1 minute. Gradually stir in milk; cook, stirring, until sauce boils and thickens. Cool 2 minutes; stir in cheeses and mustard.
5 Combine pasta, sauce and bacon in a large bowl; pour mixture into ovenproof dish. Top with breadcrumbs, dot with extra butter. Bake about 30 minutes or until browned.

prep + cook time *1 hour* **serves** *4*
nutritional count per serving *47.5g total fat (27.8g saturated fat); 3854kJ (922 cal); 78.8g carbohydrate; 43.2g protein; 3.5g fibre*

pastitsio

250g macaroni pasta
2 eggs, beaten lightly
¾ cup (60g) coarsely grated parmesan cheese
2 tablespoons stale breadcrumbs

meat sauce
2 tablespoons olive oil
2 medium brown onions (300g), chopped finely
750g beef mince
400g can tomatoes
⅓ cup (90g) tomato paste
½ cup (125ml) beef stock
¼ cup (60ml) dry white wine
½ teaspoon ground cinnamon
1 egg, beaten lightly

cheese topping
90g butter
½ cup (75g) plain flour
3½ cups (875ml) milk
1 cup (80g) coarsely grated parmesan cheese
2 egg yolks

1 Preheat oven to 180°C/160°C fan-forced. Oil shallow 2.5-litre (10-cup) ovenproof dish.
2 Make meat sauce and cheese topping.
3 Cook pasta in large saucepan of boiling water until tender; drain. Combine hot pasta, egg and cheese in large bowl. Press pasta over base of dish.
4 Top pasta evenly with meat sauce; pour over cheese topping. Smooth surface; sprinkle with breadcrumbs. Bake about 1 hour or until browned lightly. Stand 10 minutes before serving.

meat sauce Heat oil in large saucepan, add onion and beef; cook, stirring, until beef is browned. Stir in undrained crushed tomatoes, paste, stock, wine and cinnamon; simmer, uncovered, about 20 minutes or until thick. Cool; stir in egg.

cheese topping Melt butter in medium saucepan, add flour; cook, stirring, until mixture bubbles and thickens. Remove from heat; gradually stir in milk. Stir over heat until sauce boils and thickens; stir in cheese. Cool 5 minutes; stir in egg yolks.

prep + cook time *2 hours 15 minutes* **serves 6**
nutritional count per serving *45.8g total fat (22.7g saturated fat); 3528kJ (844 cal); 52.5g carbohydrate; 52.1g protein; 4.1g fibre*

chicken, spinach & ricotta bake

Use leftover chicken (diced) in soups and salads. You can also make a pie using chicken chunks.

You need half a large barbecued chicken (450g) for this recipe.

1 tablespoon olive oil
1 large brown onion (200g), chopped finely
2 cloves garlic, crushed
10 instant lasagne sheets (200g)
1½ cups (240g) shredded barbecue chicken meat
1 cup (100g) coarsely grated pizza cheese
3 cups (750ml) bottled tomato pasta sauce
2 cups (500ml) water
50g baby spinach leaves
½ cup (120g) firm ricotta cheese, crumbled

1 Heat oil in shallow flameproof dish; cook onion and garlic, stirring, until onion softens.
2 Meanwhile, break lasagne sheets into bite-sized pieces. Sprinkle pasta pieces, chicken and half the pizza cheese into the dish.
3 Pour combined pasta sauce and the water over top of chicken mixture. Simmer, covered, about 20 minutes or until pasta is tender.
4 Meanwhile, preheat grill.
5 Sprinkle bake with spinach, ricotta and remaining pizza cheese; grill about 5 minutes or until cheese melts. Stand, covered, 10 minutes before serving.
prep + cook time *50 minutes*   **serves** *4*
nutritional count per serving *18.8g total fat (7.7g saturated fat); 2195kJ (525 cal); 49.7g carbohydrate; 34.9g protein; 6.9g fibre*

spicy sausage pasta bake

375g tortiglioni pasta
6 spicy lamb sausages (900g)
1 medium brown onion (150g), chopped coarsely
1 small eggplant (230g), chopped coarsely
2 medium red capsicums (400g), chopped coarsely
3 small zucchini (270g), chopped coarsely
700g bottled tomato pasta sauce
½ cup coarsely chopped fresh basil
2 cups (200g) grated pizza cheese

1 Preheat oven to 180°C/160°C fan-forced.
2 Cook pasta in large saucepan of boiling water, uncovered, until just tender; drain.
3 Meanwhile, cook sausages in large frying pan until just cooked through. Drain on absorbent paper.
4 Cook onion, eggplant, capsicum and zucchini, stirring, in same pan until just tender.
5 Cut sausages into 2cm slices; add to vegetables in pan with sauce and basil, stir to combine.
6 Combine pasta and sausage mixture in deep 3-litre (12-cup) casserole dish; sprinkle with cheese. Bake, uncovered, about 20 minutes or until browned.
prep + cook time *50 minutes*   serves *6*
nutritional count per serving *36.3g total fat (16.5g saturated fat); 3453kJ (826 cal); 67.7g carbohydrate; 57.6g protein; 7.5g fibre*

Tortiglioni, a straight tubular pasta with grooves on the exterior, works well when baked with a chunky sauce, such as this one. You can substitute it with rigatoni or ziti, if you like, but anything less substantial will get lost amid the hearty sausage and vegetable melange.

Try to avoid going to the supermarket when you are hungry and tired – you are more likely to give in to those tempting displays.

spaghetti puttanesca

This sauce can be made 2 days ahead; refrigerate, covered, until required.

¼ cup (60ml) olive oil
2 cloves garlic, crushed
4 medium tomatoes (760g), chopped coarsely
½ cup finely chopped fresh parsley
12 stuffed olives, sliced thinly
45g can anchovy fillets, chopped finely
1 tablespoon finely shredded fresh basil
pinch chilli powder
375g spaghetti

1 Heat oil in medium frying pan; cook garlic until it just changes colour. Add tomato, parsley, olives, anchovy, basil and chilli powder; cook, stirring, 5 minutes.
2 Cook pasta in large saucepan of boiling water until tender; drain.
3 Combine sauce and pasta.
prep + cook time *30 minutes*   serves *4*
nutritional count per serving *16.9g total fat (2.5g saturated fat); 2073kJ (496 cal); 67.2g carbohydrate; 15.2g protein; 6.5g fibre*

When making a pasta sauce without cream, make enough for several servings and freeze what you do not use on the day.

spaghetti napoletana

2 x 400g cans tomatoes
30g butter
1 tablespoon olive oil
2 cloves garlic, crushed
1 tablespoon shredded fresh basil
2 tablespoons coarsely chopped
   fresh flat-leaf parsley
250g spaghetti

1 Push tomatoes, with their liquid, through sieve.
2 Heat butter and oil in large saucepan, add garlic; cook, stirring, 1 minute. Add pureed tomato; bring to the boil. Reduce heat; simmer, uncovered, about 40 minutes or until sauce reduces by about half. Stir in basil and parsley.
3 Meanwhile, cook pasta in large saucepan of boiling water, uncovered, until just tender; drain.
4 Combine sauce and pasta.
prep + cook time *55 minutes*   serves *2*
nutritional count per serving *23.7g total fat (9.6g saturated fat); 2913kJ (697 cal); 98.1g carbohydrate; 17.6g protein; 9.7g fibre*

This is the way lasagne is traditionally made in Bologna – with chicken liver and milk in the sauce. If you have the time, you can make your own pasta. This bolognese can also be served with spaghetti.

lasagne bolognese

2 teaspoons olive oil
6 slices pancetta (90g), chopped finely
1 large white onion (200g), chopped finely
1 medium carrot (120g), chopped finely
2 trimmed celery stalks (200g), chopped finely
1kg beef mince
150g chicken livers, trimmed, chopped finely
2 cups (500ml) milk
60g butter
2 cups (500ml) beef stock
1 cup (250ml) dry red wine
410g can tomato puree
2 tablespoons tomato paste
¼ cup finely chopped fresh flat-leaf parsley
6 sheets fresh lasagne (300g)
2 cups (160g) finely grated parmesan cheese

white sauce
125g butter
¾ cup (110g) plain flour
1.25 litres (5 cups) hot milk

1 Heat oil in large heavy-based pan; cook pancetta, stirring, until crisp. Add onion, carrot and celery; cook, stirring, until vegetables soften. Add beef and liver; cook, stirring, until beef just changes colour. Stir in milk and butter; cook, stirring occasionally, until liquid reduces to about half. Add stock, wine, puree and paste; simmer, uncovered, 1½ hours. Remove from heat; stir in parsley.
2 Preheat oven to 200°C/180°C fan-forced. Oil deep 26cm x 35cm baking dish.
3 Make white sauce.
4 Spread about ½ cup of the white sauce over base of dish. Layer two pasta sheets, a quarter of the meat sauce, ¼ cup of the cheese and about 1 cup of the remaining white sauce in dish. Repeat layering process, starting with pasta sheets and ending with white sauce; you will have four layers in total. Top lasagne with the remaining cheese.
5 Bake, uncovered, about 40 minutes or until top is browned lightly. Stand 15 minutes before cutting.
white sauce Melt butter in medium saucepan; add flour, stirring until mixture forms a smooth paste. Stir in milk gradually; bring to the boil, stirring, until sauce boils and thickens.
prep + cook time *4 hours (+ standing)* **serves** *8*
nutritional count per serving *44.3g total fat (26.3g saturated fat); 3269kJ (782 cal); 33.7g carbohydrate; 52.9g protein; 3.2g fibre*

Try making this recipe with some of the more exotic sausages so readily available these days (one variety with fennel and chilli is especially delicious when cooked in tomato sauce).

macaroni with
beef sausages

400g thin beef sausages
600ml bottled tomato pasta sauce
4 trimmed celery sticks (400g), chopped coarsely
1 medium green capsicum (200g), chopped coarsely
250g elbow macaroni
2 tablespoons finely chopped fresh basil leaves
1 cup (100g) coarsely grated mozzarella cheese

1 Cook sausages, in batches, in large heated frying pan until browned all over and cooked through; drain on absorbent paper, cut into 1cm slices.
2 Place sauce in same cleaned pan; bring to the boil. Add sausage, celery and capsicum; cook, stirring occasionally, about 5 minutes or until vegetables are just tender.
3 Meanwhile, cook pasta in large saucepan of boiling water, uncovered, until just tender; drain.
4 Place pasta, basil and cheese in pan with sausage and tomato sauce; toss gently to combine.
prep + cook time *30 minutes*   **serves** *4*
nutritional count per serving *33g total fat (16g saturated fat); 2863kJ (685 cal); 63.4g carbohydrate; 28.8g protein; 10g fibre*

Unlike the cream-laden carbonara that many of us are familiar with, traditional carbonara is not made with any cream. We've slightly altered the traditional carbonara recipe by adding peas; if you prefer your pasta pea-free, simply omit them from the recipe.

spaghetti carbonara
with peas

4 egg yolks
¾ cup (60g) finely grated parmesan cheese
4 rindless bacon rashers (260g), chopped finely
2 cloves garlic, sliced thinly
1 cup (120g) frozen peas
375g spaghetti

1 Combine egg yolks and cheese in small bowl.
2 Cook bacon over heat in medium frying pan about 5 minutes or until starting to crisp. Add garlic; cook, stirring, 1 minute. Add peas; cook, stirring, until heated through.
3 Meanwhile, cook pasta, uncovered, in large saucepan of boiling water until tender; drain, reserving ¼ cup cooking liquid.
4 Return pasta to saucepan. Add bacon mixture, egg mixture and reserved cooking liquid to pasta; stir over heat about 1 minute.
5 Serve with extra parmesan cheese, if you like.
prep + cook time *25 minutes*   **serves** *4*
nutritional count per serving *15.3g total fat (6.3g saturated fat); 2332kJ (558 cal); 66.8g carbohydrate; 35g protein; 5.1g fibre*

Try home brand products and compare their quality against more expensive brands. If you find no noticeable taste difference, switch to the cheaper brand.

fettuccine with creamy tomato sausage sauce

cooking-oil spray
6 thick italian sausages (480g)
2 cloves garlic, crushed
400g can crushed tomatoes
¼ cup (60ml) dry white wine
300ml cream
375g fettuccine
6 green onions, chopped finely
2 tablespoons fresh sage leaves

1 Spray large frying pan with cooking oil; cook sausages until browned all over and cooked through. Remove sausages from pan; chop coarsely. Cover to keep warm. Drain excess oil from pan.
2 Combine garlic, undrained tomatoes, wine and cream in same pan; bring to the boil. Reduce heat; simmer, uncovered, about 10 minutes or until sauce thickens slightly.
3 Meanwhile, cook pasta in large saucepan of boiling water, uncovered, until just tender; drain. Divide among serving bowls.
4 Stir sausage with onion and sage into tomato mixture; spoon sauce over pasta.

prep + cook time *40 minutes*   serves *4*
nutritional count per serving   *61.7g total fat (34.7g saturated fat); 4147kJ (992 cal); 74.8g carbohydrate; 29.6g protein; 6.9g fibre*

rigatoni with zucchini, lemon & mint

500g rigatoni pasta
¼ cup (60ml) olive oil
2 cloves garlic, crushed
3 medium zucchini (360g), grated coarsely
¾ cup (180g) ricotta cheese
1 cup coarsely chopped fresh mint
½ cup (70g) roasted slivered almonds
2 tablespoons lemon juice

1 Cook pasta in large saucepan of boiling water until just tender; drain.
2 Meanwhile, heat oil in large frying pan; cook garlic and zucchini, stirring, 2 minutes. Add cheese; cook, stirring, until just heated through.
3 Combine zucchini mixture and pasta in serving bowl with remaining ingredients.
prep + cook time *20 minutes*   **serves** 4
nutritional count per serving *30.3g total fat (6g saturated fat); 3110kJ (744 cal); 88.9g carbohydrate; 23.9g protein; 8.3g fibre*

cheesy-vegie
pasta bake

375g penne pasta

300g broccoli, cut into florets

500g cauliflower, cut into florets

2 teaspoons vegetable oil

1 large brown onion (200g), chopped finely

1 teaspoon mustard powder

1 teaspoon sweet paprika

¼ cup (35g) plain flour

1½ cups (375ml) low-fat milk

420g can tomato soup

400g can diced tomatoes

1½ cups (180g) coarsely grated reduced-fat
   cheddar cheese

2 tablespoons finely chopped
   fresh flat-leaf parsley

1 Cook pasta in large saucepan of boiling water, uncovered, until just tender; drain. Cover to keep warm.

2 Meanwhile, cook broccoli and cauliflower in medium saucepan of boiling water, uncovered, until tender; drain. Cover to keep warm.

3 Preheat grill.

4 Heat oil in same large pan; cook onion, stirring, until softened. Add mustard, paprika and flour; cook, stirring, over low heat, 2 minutes. Gradually stir in milk and soup; stir over heat until mixture boils and thickens. Add undrained tomatoes; cook, stirring, until mixture is hot.

5 Stir pasta, broccoli, cauliflower and 1 cup of the cheese into tomato mixture. Divide pasta mixture among six 1-cup (250ml) flameproof dishes, sprinkle with remaining cheese; grill until cheese melts and is browned lightly. Sprinkle pasta bake with parsley just before serving.

prep + cook time *35 minutes*   **serves** *6*
nutritional count per serving *10.9g total fat (5.4g saturated fat); 1952kJ (467 cal); 62.3g carbohydrate; 25.5g protein; 7.4g fibre*

eggplant pasta sauce

¼ cup (60ml) olive oil
1 medium brown onion (150g), chopped finely
2 trimmed celery sticks (150g), chopped finely
1 clove garlic, crushed
2 tablespoons brandy
1 medium eggplant (300g), sliced thinly
600ml bottled tomato pasta sauce
½ cup (140g) tomato paste
½ cup (125ml) water
375g rigatoni
¼ cup (20g) finely grated parmesan cheese

1 Heat oil in large saucepan; cook onion, celery and garlic, stirring, until onion softens. Add brandy; cook, stirring, until brandy evaporates. Add eggplant; cook, stirring, until eggplant is tender.
2 Stir in sauce, paste and the water; bring to the boil. Reduce heat; simmer, uncovered, about 10 minutes or until sauce thickens slightly.
3 Meanwhile, cook pasta in large saucepan of boiling water, uncovered, until just tender; drain.
4 Place pasta in large bowl with half of the eggplant sauce; toss gently to combine. Divide pasta among serving plates; top each with remaining sauce and cheese.

prep + cook time **30 minutes**   serves **4**
nutritional count per serving *17.9g total fat (3.3g saturated fat); 2625kJ (628 cal); 88.1g carbohydrate; 17.5g protein; 10.8g fibre*

pizza mexicana

1 pocket pitta bread (85g)
¼ cup (60g) canned refried beans
¼ small red capsicum (35g), chopped finely
2 teaspoons sweet chilli sauce
2 tablespoons pizza cheese
1 green onion, sliced thinly

1 Preheat oven to 180°C/160°C fan-forced.
2 Spread pitta with beans; top with capsicum, sauce and cheese. Cook about 15 minutes or until cheese melts. Sprinkle onion over pizza just before serving.
prep + cook time *20 minutes* **serves** *1*
nutritional count per serving *9.5g total fat (4.7g saturated fat); 1689kJ (404 cal); 54.7g carbohydrate; 21g protein; 6.6g fibre*

We used a small (15cm diameter) packaged pizza base for this recipe.

pizzetta caprese

1 small (112g) pizza base
2 cherry bocconcini cheeses (30g), sliced thinly
½ clove garlic, sliced thinly
1 small tomato (90g), sliced thinly
1 tablespoon fresh basil leaves

1 Preheat oven to 220°C/200°C fan-forced. Place pizza base on oven tray.
2 Place cheese and garlic on pizza base.
3 Bake about 8 minutes.
4 Serve pizzetta topped with tomato and basil.
prep + cook time *15 minutes* **serves** *1*
nutritional count per serving *9g total fat (3.6g saturated fat); 1693kJ (405 cal); 61.3g carbohydrate; 16.3g protein; 5.6g fibre*

We used large (25cm diameter) packaged pizza bases for this recipe. It's important to slice the potatoes as thinly as possible.

potato & bacon pizza

2 x large (335g) pizza bases
2 tablespoons olive oil
4 rindless bacon rashers (260g), chopped coarsely
2 cloves garlic, sliced thinly
1 tablespoon coarsely chopped fresh rosemary
½ teaspoon dried chilli flakes
500g potatoes, sliced thinly
1 cup (80g) finely grated parmesan cheese

1 Preheat oven to 220°C/200°C fan-forced. Place pizza bases on oven trays; bake about 10 minutes or until crisp.
2 Meanwhile, heat oil in large frying pan; cook bacon, garlic, rosemary and chilli, stirring, 5 minutes. Remove mixture from pan.
3 Add potato to same heated pan; cook, stirring frequently, about 10 minutes or until tender.
4 Sprinkle each pizza base with ⅓ cup of the cheese. Divide bacon mixture and potato between bases; top with remaining cheese. Bake about 5 minutes.
prep + cook time *35 minutes*   serves *4*
nutritional count per serving *25.7g total fat (7.6g saturated fat); 3486kJ (834 cal); 105.6g carbohydrate; 39.6g protein; 9g fibre*

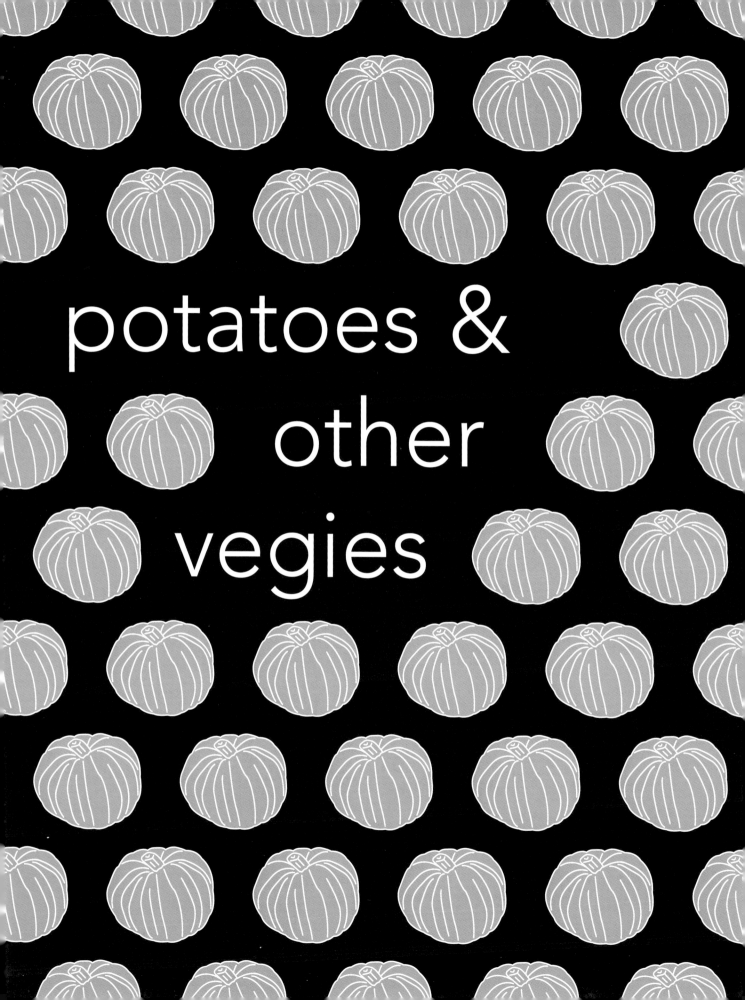

potatoes &
other
vegies

cheesy polenta with ratatouille

1 medium eggplant (300g), chopped coarsely
1 large red capsicum (350g), chopped coarsely
400g can diced tomatoes
¼ cup loosely packed fresh baby basil leaves

cheesy polenta
1.25 litres (5 cups) water
1 cup (170g) polenta
1 cup (80g) finely grated parmesan cheese

1 Cook eggplant and capsicum in heated oiled large frying pan until tender. Add undrained tomatoes; simmer, uncovered, 5 minutes or until mixture thickens slightly.
2 Meanwhile, make cheesy polenta.
3 Serve polenta with ratatouille; sprinkle with basil.
cheesy polenta Bring water to the boil in large saucepan; gradually stir in polenta. Reduce heat; cook, stirring, about 10 minutes or until polenta thickens. Remove from heat; stir in cheese. Stand 3 minutes before serving.

prep + cook time **30 minutes**   serves **4**
nutritional count per serving **7.9g total fat
(4.2g saturated fat); 1208kJ (289 cal); 37.5g
carbohydrate; 14g protein; 5.3g fibre**

pumpkin &
chickpea ratatouille

Stir ⅓ cup of loosely packed fresh basil leaves into steamed couscous for a tasty accompaniment to this ratatouille.

600g piece jap pumpkin, chopped coarsely
1 tablespoon olive oil
1 medium red onion (170g), sliced thinly
2 cloves garlic, sliced thinly
2 tablespoons tomato paste
2 tablespoons red wine vinegar
400g can crushed tomatoes
½ cup (125ml) water
1 teaspoon ground allspice
400g can chickpeas, rinsed, drained

1 Preheat oven to 220°C/200°C fan-forced.
2 Place pumpkin, in single layer, on oven tray; drizzle with half the oil. Roast, uncovered, about 20 minutes or until tender.
3 Heat remaining oil in large saucepan; cook onion and garlic, stirring, until onion softens. Add paste; cook, stirring, 1 minute. Add vinegar; cook, stirring, 1 minute. Add undrained tomatoes, the water, allspice, chickpeas and pumpkin; bring to the boil. Simmer 5 minutes.

prep + cook time *35 minutes*   **serves** *4*
nutritional count per serving *6.8g total fat (1.3g saturated fat); 899kJ (215 cal); 25.3g carbohydrate; 9.1g protein; 7.4g fibre*

When vegetables such as pumpkin, tomatoes, asparagus and cauliflower are in season, make a soup from the individual vegetable and freeze it.

fetta, avocado & roasted tomato toastie

8 x 1cm-thick slices bread, toasted
250g fetta cheese, crumbled
30g baby rocket leaves
1 medium avocado (250g), sliced thinly

roasted tomato
2 tablespoons balsamic vinegar
2 tablespoons olive oil
2 cloves garlic, crushed
8 medium egg tomatoes (600g), halved

1 Make roasted tomato.
2 Top toast with cheese, rocket, roasted tomato and avocado then drizzle with pan juices.
roasted tomato Preheat oven to 240°C/220°C fan-forced. Combine vinegar, oil and garlic in small bowl. Place tomatoes, cut-side up, in medium baking dish; drizzle with vinegar mixture. Roast about 25 minutes.
prep + cook time **40 minutes** serves **4**
nutritional count per serving **41.5g total fat (13.8g saturated fat); 2546kJ (609 cal); 37.1g carbohydrate; 19.5g protein; 6.2g fibre**

Work out which days your supermarket puts its specials on display. Stores change their pricing occasionally to attract new customers and to boost sales on specific items.

corn fritters with
cucumber salad

You need two large cobs of corn for this recipe.

1 cup (150g) self-raising flour
½ teaspoon bicarbonate of soda
1 teaspoon ground cumin
¾ cup (180ml) milk
2 eggs, separated
2 cups (330g) fresh corn kernels
2 green onions, sliced thinly
2 tablespoons finely chopped fresh coriander

cucumber salad
2 lebanese cucumbers (260g), sliced thinly
1 small red onion (100g), sliced thinly
1 fresh long red chilli, sliced thinly
⅓ cup loosely packed fresh coriander leaves
2 tablespoons sweet chilli sauce
1 tablespoon fish sauce
1 tablespoon lime juice

1 Sift flour, soda and cumin into medium bowl. Gradually whisk in milk and egg yolks until batter is smooth.
2 Beat egg whites in small bowl with electric mixer until soft peaks form. Stir corn, onion and coriander into batter; fold in egg whites.
3 Pour 2 tablespoons of the batter into heated oiled large frying pan; using metal spatula, spread batter into round shape. Cook, about 2 minutes each side or until fritter is cooked through. Remove from pan; cover to keep warm. Repeat process, wiping out pan between batches and oiling if necessary, to make a total of 18 fritters.
4 Meanwhile, make cucumber salad.
5 Serve fritters topped with salad.
cucumber salad Combine cucumber, onion, chilli and coriander in medium bowl. Place remaining ingredients in screw-top jar; shake well, drizzle over cucumber mixture.
prep + cook time *40 minutes* **serves** *6*
nutritional count per serving *4.2g total fat (1.5g saturated fat); 882kJ (211 cal); 31.8g carbohydrate; 9g protein; 4.7g fibre*

janssen's temptation

5 medium potatoes (1kg), sliced thinly
1 large brown onion (200g), sliced thinly
9 anchovy fillets, drained, halved lengthways
¼ cup (60ml) lemon juice
¾ cup (180ml) cream
2 tablespoons stale breadcrumbs
2 tablespoons finely chopped fresh flat-leaf parsley
30g butter

1 Preheat oven to 220°C/200°C fan-forced. Grease medium-deep 22cm-square baking dish.
2 Layer a third of the potato over base of dish; sprinkle over a third of the onion and a third of the anchovy. Sprinkle with 1 tablespoon of the juice. Repeat with remaining potato, onion, anchovy and juice. Pour over cream; sprinkle breadcrumbs and parsley over top then dot with butter.
3 Bake, covered, about 1 hour or until potato is tender. Uncover; bake about 15 minutes or until browned lightly.
prep + cook time *1 hour 30 minutes* **serves 4**
nutritional count per serving *26.5g total fat (17.1g saturated fat); 1868kJ (447 cal); 39.2g carbohydrate; 10.5g protein; 6g fibre*

This is our take on the traditional Swedish recipe of the same name. Even if you're not a lover of anchovies, we're certain you'll love this dish. Try serving this dish with a green salad, dressed with a lemon vinaigrette.

bacon & potato hash

8 rindless bacon rashers (500g)
3 medium potatoes (600g), cut into 1cm pieces
1 large red capsicum (350g), chopped coarsely
5g butter
3 shallots (75g), chopped coarsely
½ teaspoon smoked paprika

lemon vinaigrette
1 teaspoon dijon mustard
2 tablespoons lemon juice
1 tablespoon olive oil

1 Cook bacon in heated large frying pan, in batches, until beginning to crisp. Coarsely chop half the bacon; keep warm.
2 Meanwhile, boil, steam or microwave potato and capsicum, separately, until almost tender; drain well.
3 Make lemon vinaigrette.
4 Melt butter in same frying pan; add potato, cook, stirring occasionally, about 10 minutes or until browned lightly. Add shallot, paprika, chopped bacon and capsicum; cook, stirring, until shallot softens. Remove from heat; drizzle with vinaigrette.
5 Serve hash topped with remaining bacon.
lemon vinaigrette Place ingredients in screw-top jar; shake well.

prep + cook time *35 minutes* **serves** *4*
nutritional count per serving *12.8g total fat (3.8g saturated fat); 1454kJ (348 cal); 24.1g carbohydrate; 31.8g protein; 4g fibre*

Perfect for breakfast, lunch or dinner, this recipe can easily be doubled to feed a starving army of kids. Poached or fried eggs complement this recipe well, as does a side serving of toast.

Always buy the form of the product that best suits the dish you are making. For example, tuna flakes are good for a salad.

warm potato & broad bean salad with tuna

A grilled tuna steak would also taste terrific in place of the canned tuna in this salad. Peas or snow peas can be used instead of the broad beans.

10 small potatoes (1.2kg), sliced thickly
¼ cup (60ml) olive oil
2 tablespoons wholegrain mustard
1 tablespoon white wine vinegar
2 tablespoons lemon juice
½ small red onion (50g), sliced thinly
425g tuna in springwater, drained, flaked
500g frozen broad beans

1 Boil, steam or microwave potato until tender; drain.
2 Whisk oil, mustard, vinegar and juice in small bowl.
3 Combine potato in large bowl with dressing, onion and tuna.
4 Meanwhile, boil, steam or microwave beans until just tender. Peel; discard shell. Add beans to potato salad; toss gently to combine.

prep + cook time *30 minutes* serves *4*
nutritional count per serving *16.7g total fat (2.8g saturated fat); 2190kJ (524 cal); 49.9g carbohydrate; 35.2g protein; 15.7g fibre*

warm potato
& beetroot salad

For nicely crisped potatoes, heat the oven tray before adding the potatoes. You can sprinkle ¼ cup chopped fresh chives over the salad just before serving.

5 medium potatoes (1kg), halved
¼ cup (60ml) olive oil
2 tablespoons balsamic vinegar
½ small red onion (50g), chopped finely
¼ cup (50g) rinsed, drained baby capers
850g can baby beetroot, drained, quartered
3 hard-boiled eggs, quartered

1 Preheat oven to 220°C/200°C fan-forced.
2 Cook potato in large saucepan of boiling water 5 minutes; drain. Cut potato into wedges, combine with 1 tablespoon of the oil on oven tray. Roast, uncovered, about 45 minutes or until potato is browned lightly.
3 Meanwhile, whisk vinegar and remaining oil in small bowl.
4 Place potato in large bowl with onion, capers and beetroot; drizzle with dressing. Top salad with egg; serve warm.

prep + cook time *55 minutes* **serves** *4*
nutritional count per serving *18g total fat (3.1g saturated fat); 1777kJ (425 cal); 48g carbohydrate; 13.2g protein; 9.1g fibre*

A large pottery urn filled with soil is ideal if you want to grow potatoes in a courtyard garden. Ask your local seed retailer for the best type to grow in a pot. When ready, you will have fresh new potatoes at your fingertips.

baked potatoes

The perfect baked potato should be salty and crisp on the outside and snow white and fluffy on the inside. You can also use russet burbank or spunta potatoes for this recipe.

8 king edward potatoes (1.4kg), unpeeled

1 Preheat oven to 180°C/160°C fan-forced.
2 Pierce skin of each potato with fork; wrap each potato in foil, place on oven tray. Bake about 1 hour or until tender.
3 Top potatoes with one of the suggested toppings.
prep + cook time *1 hour 5 minutes* makes *8*
nutritional count per potato *0.2g total fat (0g saturated fat); 493kJ (118 cal); 22.9g carbohydrate; 4.29g protein; 3.5g fibre*

toppings

prep time *5 minutes*   serves *8*

cream cheese & pesto Combine ⅔ cup spreadable cream cheese, ⅓ cup pesto and ½ teaspoon cracked black pepper in small bowl; refrigerate until required.
nutrition count per potato *11.3g total fat (5.2g saturated fat); 966kJ (231 cal); 23.6g carbohydrate; 7g protein; 3.8g fibre*

lime & chilli yogurt Combine ⅔ cup yogurt, 2 tablespoons coarsely chopped fresh coriander, 2 fresh small seeded finely chopped red thai chillies and 1 teaspoon finely grated lime rind in small bowl; refrigerate until required.
nutrition count per potato *1g total fat (0.5g saturated fat); 564kJ (135 cal); 24.1g carbohydrate; 5.3g protein; 3.5g fibre*

mustard & walnut butter Mash 60g softened butter, 1 teaspoon wholegrain mustard and 2 tablespoons finely chopped roasted walnuts in small bowl until mixture forms a paste; refrigerate until required.
nutrition count per potato *7.9g total fat (4.1g saturated fat); 790kJ (189 cal); 23.1g carbohydrate; 4.6g protein; 3.7g fibre*

potato & tuna bake

You could also make this recipe in a 1-litre (4-cup) baking dish.

3 medium potatoes (600g), cut into 1cm pieces
20g butter
1 tablespoon olive oil
3 shallots (75g), chopped coarsely
425g can tuna in oil, drained
250g frozen spinach, thawed, drained
½ cup (125ml) milk
1½ cups (180g) coarsely grated cheddar cheese
½ cup (75g) drained semi-dried tomatoes, chopped coarsely

1 Preheat oven to 220°C/200°C fan-forced. Oil four 1-cup (250ml) shallow baking dishes.
2 Boil, steam or microwave potato until almost tender; drain.
3 Heat butter and oil in large frying pan; add potato, cook, stirring occasionally, about 10 minutes or until browned lightly. Add shallot; cook, stirring, until shallot softens. Transfer mixture to medium bowl; coarsely crush potato mixture with fork.
4 Stir tuna, spinach, milk, ½ cup of the cheese and tomatoes into potato mixture. Divide mixture among dishes; sprinkle with remaining cheese. Bake, uncovered, about 10 minutes or until browned lightly.
prep + cook time **40 minutes**   serves **4**
nutritional count per serving **38.8g total fat (15.9g saturated fat); 2696kJ (645 cal); 28.6g carbohydrate; 41.5g protein; 8.8g fibre**

potato & pea curry

3 medium potatoes (600g), chopped coarsely
1 tablespoon vegetable oil
2 cloves garlic, crushed
2cm piece fresh ginger (10g), grated
¼ cup (75g) tikka masala curry paste
300ml cream
1½ cups (180g) frozen peas
½ cup (140g) yogurt
2 tablespoons lime juice
4 small pappadums
4 hard-boiled eggs, halved

1 Boil, steam or microwave potato until just tender; drain.
2 Meanwhile, heat oil in large saucepan; cook garlic and ginger, stirring, 2 minutes. Add paste; cook, stirring, until fragrant.
3 Add cream, bring to the boil; reduce heat. Add potato; simmer, uncovered, 5 minutes. Add peas and yogurt; stir over low heat about 5 minutes or until peas are heated through. Stir in juice.
4 Cook pappadums, in microwave oven, following packet instructions.
5 Top curry with egg; serve with pappadums.
prep + cook time **40 minutes** serves **4**
nutritional count per serving *51.8g total fat (25.5g saturated fat); 3106kJ (743 cal); 37.8g carbohydrate; 22.7g protein; 24.5g fibre*

Mashed potato, cream and cheese, what else do you need? One spoonful of this delectable dish and the answer will most certainly be "nothing". You can also use pink-eye or sebago potatoes for this recipe.

potatoes byron

1kg russet burbank potatoes, unpeeled
60g butter, chopped
½ cup (125ml) cream
¼ cup (20g) finely grated parmesan cheese
¼ cup (30g) finely grated gruyère cheese

1 Preheat oven to 180°C/160°C fan-forced. Oil four shallow 1-cup (250ml) ovenproof dishes.
2 Pierce skin of each potato with fork; place on oven tray. Bake, uncovered, about 1 hour or until tender. Cover; cool 10 minutes.
3 Split potatoes in half lengthways; scoop flesh into medium bowl, discard potato skins. Mash potato with butter.
4 Divide potato among dishes. Pour cream evenly over potato; sprinkle with combined cheeses. Bake, uncovered, about 10 minutes or until heated through and browned lightly.

prep + cook time *1 hour 20 minutes (+ cooling)*
serves *4*
nutritional count per serving *30.2g total fat (19.7g saturated fat); 1910kJ (457 cal); 33.8g carbohydrate; 10.8g protein; 5g fibre*

The combination of mashed potato, bacon, onion, cheese and sour cream in these cakes is so good you'll find it hard to stop at one. You can also use lasoda or pink-eye potatoes for this recipe.

potato cakes

1kg sebago potatoes, peeled, chopped coarsely
4 green onions, sliced thinly
4 rindless bacon rashers (260g), chopped finely
⅓ cup (40g) coarsely grated cheddar cheese
2 tablespoons sour cream
½ cup (75g) plain flour
50g butter
2 tablespoons olive oil

1 Boil, steam or microwave potato until tender; drain. Mash potato in large bowl until smooth.
2 Meanwhile, cook onion and bacon in small frying pan, stirring, until bacon is crisp. Add bacon mixture to potato with cheese and sour cream; stir to combine.
3 Using floured hands, shape potato mixture into 12 patties; roll in flour, shake off excess.
4 Heat butter and oil in large frying pan; cook potato cakes, in batches, until browned lightly both sides. Serve with lemon wedges, if desired.
prep + cook time *45 minutes* **makes** *12*
nutritional count per cake *11.9g total fat (5.3g saturated fat); 823kJ (197 cal); 14.1g carbohydrate; 7.6g protein; 1.4g fibre*

Chickpeas are cheaper to purchase dried rather than canned – soak overnight for use the following day. Leftover chickpeas can be added to salads or soups, or made into a spread for sandwiches.

chickpea & vegetable braise

1 cup (200g) dried chickpeas
2 tablespoons olive oil
2 small leeks (400g), chopped coarsely
2 medium carrots (240g), cut into batons
2 cloves garlic, crushed
1 tablespoon finely chopped fresh rosemary
2 tablespoons white wine vinegar
2 cups (500ml) vegetable stock
100g baby spinach leaves
¼ cup (60ml) lemon juice
2 tablespoons olive oil, extra
2 cloves garlic, crushed, extra

cumin couscous
1 cup (250ml) boiling water
1 cup (200g) couscous
1 tablespoon olive oil
1 teaspoon ground cumin

1 Place chickpeas in medium bowl, cover with cold water; stand overnight, drain. Rinse under cold water; drain. Place chickpeas in medium saucepan of boiling water. Return to the boil, reduce heat; simmer, uncovered, about 40 minutes or until chickpeas are tender. Drain.
2 Meanwhile, preheat oven to 160°C/140°C fan-forced.
3 Heat oil in large deep flameproof baking dish; cook leek and carrot, stirring, until just tender. Add garlic, rosemary and chickpeas; cook, stirring, until fragrant. Add vinegar and stock; bring to the boil. Cover; cook in oven 30 minutes.
4 Meanwhile, make cumin couscous.
5 Remove dish from oven; stir in spinach, juice, extra oil and extra garlic. Serve chickpea and vegetable braise with couscous.
cumin couscous Combine the water and couscous in medium heatproof bowl, cover; stand about 5 minutes or until liquid is absorbed, fluffing with fork occasionally. Add oil and cumin; toss gently to combine.
prep + cook time *1 hour 45 minutes (+ standing)* **serves** *4*
nutritional count per serving *26.9g total fat (3.9g saturated fat); 2483kJ (594 cal); 63.2g carbohydrate; 19g protein; 11.4g fibre*

red beans & rice

2 rindless bacon rashers (130g), chopped coarsely
1 medium brown onion (150g), chopped finely
1 small red capsicum (150g), chopped finely
2 cloves garlic, crushed
1 tablespoon tomato paste
1 tablespoon red wine vinegar
1 teaspoon smoked paprika
2 cups (400g) white long-grain rice
1 bay leaf
1 cup (250ml) chicken stock
2¼ cups (560ml) water
400g can kidney beans, rinsed, drained
½ cup (80g) frozen corn kernels
1 tablespoon lime juice

1 Cook bacon in a heated large frying pan, stirring, until starting to crisp. Add onion, capsicum and garlic; cook, stirring until capsicum softens.
2 Add paste, vinegar and paprika; cook, stirring, 1 minute. Add rice; cook, stirring, 2 minutes.
3 Add bay leaf, stock, the water and beans, bring to the boil; reduce heat, simmer, covered, 20 minutes. Add corn; cook, covered, about 5 minutes or until rice is tender. Remove from heat; stand, covered, 5 minutes. Stir in juice.
prep + cook time *1 hour*   **serves** *4*
nutritional count per serving *3.3g total fat (1g saturated fat); 2215kJ (530 cal); 99.3g carbohydrate; 20.8g protein; 7.1g fibre*

Typical Southern food in the USA, red beans and rice is a filling and budget-friendly dish. If you like, serve with grilled chicken for a meatier meal.

falafel

2 x 400g cans chickpeas, rinsed, drained
1 clove garlic, chopped coarsely
1 small brown onion (80g), chopped coarsely
1 tablespoon olive oil
1 egg
2 teaspoons ground cumin
½ teaspoon bicarbonate of soda
2 tablespoons plain flour
vegetable oil, for shallow-frying
4 large pitta breads (320g), warmed

yogurt sauce
1 cup (280g) yogurt
½ clove garlic, crushed
1 tablespoon lemon juice
½ teaspoon cayenne pepper

1 Process chickpeas, garlic, onion and olive oil until ingredients begin to combine; transfer mixture to medium bowl. Stir in egg, cumin, soda and flour until combined. Shape mixture into 12 patties.
2 Heat vegetable oil in large frying pan; cook felafel, in batches, until browned. Drain on absorbent paper.
3 Meanwhile, make yogurt sauce.
4 Serve felafel on pitta, topped with yogurt sauce. You can serve the felafel with a rocket and tomato salad, if you like.
yogurt sauce Combine ingredients in small bowl.
prep + cook time **25 minutes** serves **4**
nutritional count per serving **21.8g total fat (4.3g saturated fat); 2416kJ (575 cal); 68.3g carbohydrate; 21.7g protein; 9.1g fibre**

It's important that you measure the bicarbonate of soda exactly, otherwise you will find that the felafel is tainted with the taste of excess soda. It's a good idea to sift the soda as it's often lumpy. Hummus also tastes great with felafel.

Buy fresh local produce at farmers' markets. Not only are the fruit and vegetables fresher, they will last longer. Markets can also be cheaper than the supermarket. There is often a wider range of different varieties available as some stalls may specialise in unusual varieties – such as egglant or tomatoes – you can't find elsewhere.

tofu &
vegetable curry

300g firm silken tofu

6 cloves garlic, quartered

3 fresh small red thai chillies, chopped coarsely

10cm stick fresh lemon grass (20g),
 chopped coarsely

4cm piece fresh ginger (20g), chopped coarsely

1.5cm piece fresh turmeric (20g), chopped coarsely

1 medium brown onion (150g), chopped finely

1 tablespoon vegetable oil

400ml can coconut milk

1 cup (250ml) vegetable stock

2 fresh kaffir lime leaves

4 medium zucchini (480g), chopped coarsely

1 small cauliflower (1kg), cut into florets

1 tablespoon soy sauce

1 tablespoon lime juice

⅓ cup firmly packed fresh coriander,
 chopped coarsely

¼ cup loosely packed fresh thai basil leaves

1 Press tofu between two chopping boards with a weight on top, raise one end; stand 10 minutes. Cut tofu into 2cm cubes; pat dry between layers of absorbent paper.

2 Blend or process garlic, chilli, lemon grass, ginger, turmeric, onion and oil until mixture forms a paste.

3 Cook garlic paste in large saucepan, stirring, 5 minutes. Add coconut milk, stock and lime leaves; simmer, uncovered, stirring occasionally, 10 minutes.

4 Add zucchini and cauliflower; simmer, uncovered, about 5 minutes or until vegetables are tender.

5 Discard lime leaves; stir in tofu, sauce, juice and coriander. Sprinkle with basil before serving.

prep + cook time *50 minutes*   serves *4*
nutritional count per serving *31.7g total fat (19.7g saturated fat); 1843kJ (441 cal); 14.8g carbohydrate; 19.8g protein; 11g fibre*

mixed dhal

2 tablespoons ghee
1 medium brown onion (150g), chopped finely
2 cloves garlic, crushed
4cm piece fresh ginger (20g), grated
1½ tablespoons black mustard seeds
1 long green chilli, chopped finely
1 tablespoon ground cumin
1 tablespoon ground coriander
2 teaspoons ground turmeric
½ cup (100g) brown lentils
⅓ cup (65g) red lentils
⅓ cup (85g) yellow split peas
⅓ cup (85g) green split peas
400g can crushed tomatoes
2 cups (500ml) vegetable stock
1½ cups (375ml) water
140ml can coconut cream

1 Heat ghee in large saucepan; cook onion, garlic and ginger, stirring, until onion softens. Add seeds, chilli and spices; cook, stirring, until fragrant.
2 Add lentils and peas to pan. Stir in undrained tomatoes, stock and the water; simmer, covered, stirring occasionally, about 1 hour or until lentils are tender.
3 Just before serving, add coconut cream; stir over low heat until curry is heated through.

prep + cook time *1 hour 25 minutes*   serves *4*
nutritional count per serving *18.4g total fat (12.5g saturated fat); 1898kJ (454 cal); 42.6g carbohydrate; 23.3g protein; 12.7g fibre*

The word dhal is the Hindi word for legumes and pulses; regarded as meat substitutes, they feature widely in Indian cooking because they are a good source of protein for this largely vegetarian nation.

jambalaya

1 tablespoon olive oil
4 smoked chorizo sausages (680g)
400g chicken breast fillets
1 medium red onion (170g), chopped finely
1 medium red capsicum (200g), chopped finely
2 cloves garlic, crushed
2 tablespoons finely chopped bottled
    jalapeño chillies
1 teaspoon dried oregano
¼ teaspoon cayenne pepper
1 bay leaf
2 tablespoons tomato paste
1½ cups (300g) white long-grain rice
400g can crushed tomatoes
2 cups (500ml) chicken stock

1 Heat oil in large saucepan; cook sausages, turning occasionally, until browned. Remove from pan; slice thickly. Add chicken to pan; cook, turning occasionally, until browned. Remove from pan; slice thickly.

2 Cook onion, capsicum and garlic in same pan, stirring, until capsicum softens. Add chilli; cook, stirring, 1 minute. Add spices, bay leaf and paste; cook, stirring, 2 minutes. Add rice; stir to coat in mixture.

3 Add undrained tomatoes and stock, bring to a simmer; return sausage and chicken to pan. Cook, covered, about 45 minutes or until rice is tender and liquid absorbed.

prep + cook time *1 hour 30 minutes* serves *4*
nutritional count per serving *62.3g total fat (21.2g saturated fat); 4648kJ (1112 cal); 73g carbohydrate; 63.3g protein; 4.5g fibre*

This dish is a real one-pot-wonder, very similar to the Spanish staple, paella: jambalaya is the US-version and, like paella, often contains seafood.

pumpkin & eggplant dhal

2 tablespoons olive oil
1 medium brown onion (150g), sliced thinly
2 cloves garlic, crushed
4cm piece fresh ginger (20g), grated
2 teaspoons ground cumin
2 teaspoons ground coriander
1 teaspoon ground turmeric
⅓ cup (65g) red lentils
⅓ cup (85g) yellow split peas
⅓ cup (85g) green split peas
410g can crushed tomatoes
1½ cups (375ml) vegetable stock
2 cups (500ml) water
300g piece pumpkin, chopped coarsely
1 medium eggplant (300g), chopped coarsely
400g can chickpeas, rinsed, drained

1 Heat oil in large saucepan; cook onion, garlic and ginger, stirring, until onion softens. Add spices; cook, stirring, until fragrant.
2 Add lentils and peas to pan. Stir in undrained tomatoes, stock and the water; simmer, covered, stirring occasionally, 30 minutes. Add pumpkin and eggplant; bring to the boil. Reduce heat; simmer, covered, about 20 minutes or until pumpkin is tender. Add chickpeas, simmer 10 minutes.
prep + cook time *1 hour 30 minutes* **serves** *4*
nutritional count per serving *12.9g total fat (2g saturated fat); 1793kJ (429 cal); 48.1g carbohydrate; 22.8g protein; 14.4g fibre*

creamed spinach, kumara & potato gratin

10g butter
1 teaspoon olive oil
1 medium brown onion (150g), chopped finely
2 x 250g packets frozen spinach, thawed, drained
300ml cream
¾ cup (180ml) milk
1 large kumara (500g), sliced thinly
2 large potatoes (600g), sliced thinly
⅓ cup (25g) coarsely grated parmesan cheese

1 Preheat oven to 220°C/200°C fan-forced.
Oil deep medium 25cm x 30cm baking dish.
2 Melt butter with oil in medium frying pan,
add onion; cook, stirring, until onion softens.
Add spinach, ½ cup of the cream and ½ cup of
the milk; cook, stirring, 2 minutes.
3 Place a third of the kumara and a third of the
potato, slightly overlapping, in dish; spread with
half the spinach mixture. Repeat layering, ending
with kumara and potato. Pour over remaining
combined cream and milk; sprinkle with cheese.
4 Bake, covered, about 1 hour or until potato is
tender. Uncover; bake about 10 minutes or until
browned lightly.

prep + cook time *1 hour 45 minutes* serves 6
nutritional count per serving *26.7g total fat
(16.9g saturated fat); 1655kJ (396 cal); 27.6g
carbohydrate; 9.2g protein; 5.7g fibre*

chickpea &
vegetable gratin

You could also cook and serve this in individual ramekins. Use six 2-cup (500ml) ovenproof dishes instead of a 2.5-litre (10-cup) dish in step 5.

2 tablespoons olive oil

1 large brown onion (200g), chopped finely

4 cloves garlic, crushed

½ teaspoon ground allspice

½ teaspoon chilli flakes

2 x 400g cans diced tomatoes

2 large red capsicums (700g)

2 medium eggplants (600g), cut into 5mm slices

3 medium zucchini (360g), cut into 5mm slices

2 x 400g cans chickpeas, rinsed, drained

½ cup coarsely chopped fresh flat-leaf parsley

⅓ cup coarsely chopped fresh basil

1 teaspoon fresh thyme leaves

1 teaspoon white sugar

1 cup (80g) finely grated parmesan cheese

1 Preheat grill.

2 Heat half the oil in medium saucepan; cook onion, stirring, until softened. Add garlic, allspice and chilli; cook, stirring, until fragrant. Add undrained tomatoes; simmer, uncovered, about 15 minutes or until sauce thickens slightly.

3 Meanwhile, quarter capsicums; discard seeds and membranes. Roast under grill or in very hot oven, skin-side up, until skin blisters and blackens. Cover capsicum pieces with plastic or paper 5 minutes; peel away skin then cut capsicum into 3cm pieces.

4 Combine eggplant, zucchini and remaining oil in large bowl; place vegetables on two oven trays, grill both sides until tender.

5 Preheat oven to 200°C/180°C fan-forced.

6 Stir chickpeas, herbs and sugar into tomato sauce. Place half the combined capsicum, eggplant and zucchini in shallow 2.5-litre (10-cup) ovenproof dish; pour half the chickpea sauce over vegetables. Repeat layering; sprinkle with cheese. Bake, uncovered, about 20 minutes or until browned lightly.

prep + cook time *1 hour* serves *6*
nutritional count per serving *13.3g total fat (3.9g saturated fat); 1296kJ (310 cal); 26.4g carbohydrate; 15.8g protein; 11.2g fibre*

chickpeas in spicy tomato sauce

This recipe gets its heat from the cayenne, the ground dried pods of a special variety of pungent chilli. Vegetarians will be delighted with the chickpeas as a main course served with raita, and Indian breads such as chapati or paratha.

2 tablespoons ghee
2 teaspoons cumin seeds
2 medium brown onions (300g), chopped finely
2 cloves garlic, crushed
4cm piece fresh ginger (20g), grated
1 tablespoon ground coriander
1 teaspoon ground turmeric
1 teaspoon cayenne pepper
2 tablespoons tomato paste
2 x 400g cans diced tomatoes
2 cups (500ml) water
2 x 420g cans chickpeas, rinsed, drained
1 large kumara (500g), cut into 1.5cm pieces
300g spinach, trimmed, chopped coarsely

1 Heat ghee in large saucepan; cook seeds, stirring, until fragrant. Add onion, garlic and ginger; cook, stirring, until onion softens. Add spices; cook, stirring, until fragrant. Add tomato paste; cook, stirring, 2 minutes.
2 Add undrained tomatoes, the water, chickpeas and kumara; simmer, covered, stirring occasionally, about 30 minutes or until kumara is tender and mixture thickens slightly.
3 Stir in spinach just before serving.
prep + cook time *1 hour* **serves** *6*
nutritional count per serving *8.1g total fat (4.1g saturated fat); 1037kJ (248 cal); 29.1g carbohydrate; 9.9g protein; 9.4g fibre*

vegetable tagine with split peas

2 tablespoons olive oil
1 large red onion (300g), sliced thinly
¾ cup (150g) yellow split peas
2 cloves garlic, crushed
5cm piece fresh ginger (25g), grated
3 teaspoons ground coriander
2 teaspoons ground cumin
2 teaspoons sweet paprika
1 teaspoon caraway seeds
1 litre (4 cups) vegetable stock
400g can diced tomatoes
750g butternut pumpkin, cut into 2cm pieces
350g yellow patty pan squash, quartered
200g green beans, trimmed, halved widthways
½ cup (125ml) water
½ cup coarsely chopped fresh coriander

1 Heat oil in large saucepan; cook onion, stirring, until softened. Add peas, garlic, ginger, spices and seeds; cook, stirring, until fragrant.
2 Add stock and undrained tomatoes; bring to the boil. Reduce heat; simmer, uncovered, stirring occasionally, 15 minutes. Add pumpkin; simmer about 15 minutes or until peas are tender. Stir in squash, beans and the water, cover; cook about 5 minutes or until vegetables are tender.
3 Serve tagine sprinkled with chopped coriander. Accompany with thick yogurt flavoured with grated lemon rind, if you like.

prep + cook time *1 hour* serves *6*
nutritional count per serving *8.3g total fat (1.6g saturated fat); 1070kJ (256 cal); 27.8g carbohydrate; 13.5g protein; 7.9g fibre*

Cook the tagine up to the stage where the split peas are tender (step 2), several hours ahead if you like. Prepare the vegetables ahead of time, ready to add to the tagine for the last cooking stage. This way you'll retain the colours of the vegetables.

canned &
fresh fish

tuna mornay

30g butter
1 medium brown onion (150g), chopped finely
1 trimmed celery stalk (100g), chopped finely
1 tablespoon plain flour
¾ cup (180ml) milk
½ cup (125ml) cream
⅓ cup (40g) grated cheddar cheese
130g can corn kernels, drained
2 x 185g can tuna, drained
1 cup (70g) stale breadcrumbs
¼ cup (30g) grated cheddar cheese, extra

1 Preheat oven to 180°C/160°C fan-forced.
2 Melt butter in medium saucepan; cook onion and celery, stirring, until onion is soft. Add flour; cook, stirring, 1 minute. Gradually stir in combined milk and cream; cook, stirring, until mixture boils and thickens. Remove pan from heat, add cheese, corn and tuna; stir until cheese is melted.
3 Spoon mornay mixture into four 1½-cup (375ml) ovenproof dishes. Sprinkle with combined breadcrumbs and extra cheese.
4 Bake tuna mornay about 15 minutes or until heated through.
prep + cook time *10 minutes* **serves 4**
nutritional count per serving *30.2g total fat (18.8g saturated fat); 2031kJ (486 cal); 23.4g carbohydrate; 29.3g protein; 2.5g fibre*

We used sebago potatoes in this recipe, but you can also use lasoda, coliban, nicola or pink-eye, if you like.

salmon & green bean
potato patties

150g green beans
800g potatoes, chopped coarsely
20g butter
⅓ cup (25g) finely grated parmesan cheese
1 egg
415g can red salmon
⅓ cup (35g) packaged breadcrumbs
vegetable oil, for shallow-frying
150g baby spinach leaves
1 medium lemon (140g), cut into wedges

1 Boil, steam or microwave beans until tender; drain. Rinse under cold water; drain. Chop coarsely.
2 Boil, steam or microwave potato until tender; drain. Mash potato in large bowl with butter, cheese and egg until smooth.
3 Drain salmon; discard skin and bones. Add salmon and beans to potato mixture; mix well. Shape salmon mixture into 12 patties; coat in breadcrumbs. Place patties on tray, cover; refrigerate 30 minutes.
4 Heat oil in large frying pan; fry patties, in batches, until browned lightly and heated through. Drain on absorbent paper; serve on spinach with lemon wedges.
prep + cook time *50 minutes (+ refrigeration)*
serves **4**
nutritional count per serving *51.7g total fat (8.7g saturated fat); 2959kJ (708 cal); 29.6g carbohydrate; 29.5g protein; 5.6g fibre*

You can also use coliban or nicola potatoes for this recipe. Patties can be prepared a day ahead; cover and refrigerate until required.

perfect salmon patties

1kg lasoda potatoes, peeled
440g can red salmon
1 small brown onion (80g), chopped finely
1 tablespoon finely chopped fresh flat-leaf parsley
1 teaspoon finely grated lemon rind
1 tablespoon lemon juice
½ cup (75g) plain flour
1 egg
2 tablespoons milk
½ cup (50g) packaged breadcrumbs
½ cup (35g) stale breadcrumbs
vegetable oil, for deep-frying

1 Boil, steam or microwave potatoes until tender; drain. Mash potato in large bowl.
2 Drain salmon; discard any skin and bones. Add salmon to potato with onion, parsley, rind and juice; mix well. Cover; refrigerate 30 minutes.
3 Using floured hands, shape salmon mixture into eight patties. Toss patties in flour; shake away excess. Dip patties, one at a time, in combined egg and milk, then in combined breadcrumbs.
4 Heat oil in wok or large saucepan; deep-fry patties, in batches, until browned lightly. Drain.
prep + cook time *40 minutes (+ refrigeration)*
makes *8*
nutritional count per patty *8.2g total fat (1.5g saturated fat); 681kJ (163 cal); 14g carbohydrate; 7.8g protein; 1.3g fibre*

If you have the time, buy fresh whole fish and fillet it yourself, using the head, bones and tails to make fish stock.

classic fish & chips

Reheat the oil between frying batches of chips and fish.

1 cup (150g) self-raising flour
1 cup (250ml) dry ale
1 tablespoon sea salt
1kg potatoes, peeled
peanut oil, for deep-frying
4 x 150g blue-eye fillets, halved lengthways

tartare sauce
⅔ cup (200g) whole-egg mayonnaise
½ small brown onion (40g), chopped finely
2 tablespoons finely chopped cornichons
1 tablespoon drained capers, rinsed,
    chopped finely
1 tablespoon finely chopped fresh
    flat-leaf parsley
1 tablespoon lemon juice

1 Make tartare sauce.
2 Sift flour into medium bowl; whisk in beer and salt until smooth.
3 Cut potatoes lengthways into 1cm slices; cut each slice lengthways into 1cm-chips; dry with absorbent paper.
4 Heat oil in large saucepan. Cook chips, in three batches, about 2 minutes or until tender but not brown. Drain on absorbent paper.
5 Dip fish in batter; drain away excess. Deep-fry fish, in batches, until cooked. Drain on absorbent paper.
6 Deep-fry chips, in three batches, until crisp and golden brown; drain on absorbent paper. Serve fish and chips with sauce and lemon wedges, if you like.
tartare sauce Combine ingredients in medium bowl.
prep + cook time *55 minutes* **serves** *4*
nutritional count per serving *38.3g total fat (6.2g saturated fat); 3340kJ (799 cal); 66.1g carbohydrate; 40.3g protein; 5.4g fibre*

tuna spinach
mornay pie with mash

50g butter
1 medium brown onion (150g), sliced thinly
¼ cup (35g) plain flour
2 cups (500ml) milk, warmed
150g baby spinach leaves
425g can tuna in springwater, drained
2 tablespoons lemon juice

potato & celeriac mash
400g potatoes, chopped coarsely
300g celeriac, chopped coarsely
2 tablespoons milk
30g butter
¼ cup (20g) finely grated parmesan cheese

1 Make potato and celeriac mash.
2 Melt butter in medium saucepan; cook onion, stirring, about 5 minutes or until softened. Add flour; cook, stirring, until mixture thickens and bubbles. Gradually add milk; stir until mixture boils and thickens. Remove from heat; stir in spinach, tuna and juice.
3 Preheat grill.
4 Spoon tuna mixture into shallow flameproof 1.5 litre (6-cup) dish; top with mash. Grill until browned lightly.
potato & celeriac mash Boil, steam or microwave potato and celeriac, separately, until tender; drain. Combine potato and celeriac in large bowl; mash with milk and butter until smooth. Stir in cheese; cover to keep warm.
prep + cook time *50 minutes* **serves** *4*
nutritional count per serving *25.8g total fat (12.1g saturated fat); 2040kJ (488 cal); 29.7g carbohydrate; 31.7g protein; 5.8g fibre*

combination fried rice

You need to cook 1⅓ cups of white long-grain rice the day before you make this dish; spread cooled rice on a tray, cover and refrigerate overnight.

300g uncooked small king prawns
¼ cup (60ml) peanut oil
400g chicken breast fillets, sliced thinly
3 eggs, beaten lightly
4 rindless bacon rashers (260g), chopped coarsely
1 medium brown onion (150g), chopped finely
1 medium red capsicum (200g), chopped finely
2 cloves garlic, crushed
3cm piece fresh ginger (15g), grated
3 cups cooked white long-grain rice
2 tablespoons light soy sauce
¾ cup (90g) frozen peas
3 green onions, sliced thinly

1 Shell and devein prawns, leaving tails intact.
2 Heat 1 tablespoon of the oil in wok; stir-fry chicken, in batches, until cooked. Stir-fry prawns, in batches, until changed in colour.
3 Heat half the remaining oil in wok; stir-fry egg until just set then remove from wok.
4 Heat remaining oil in wok; stir-fry bacon, brown onion, capsicum, garlic and ginger until bacon is crisp. Return chicken, prawns and egg to wok with remaining ingredients; stir-fry until hot.

prep + cook time *40 minutes*   **serves** *4*
nutritional count per serving *35.1g total fat (9.4g saturated fat); 3001kJ (718 cal); 46.5g carbohydrate; 52.3g protein; 3.9g fibre*

Buy fish when they are in ample supply – they'll be cheaper. Check with your local fish store or online for when the fish you want is available.

smoked fish pot pies

You can also use lasoda or nicola potatoes in this recipe.

750g smoked cod fillets
2 cups (500ml) milk
1 bay leaf
6 black peppercorns
1kg coliban potatoes, peeled, chopped coarsely
50g butter, softened
20g butter, extra
1 large brown onion (200g), chopped finely
1 clove garlic, crushed
¼ cup (35g) plain flour
2½ cups (625ml) milk, extra
1 cup (120g) frozen peas
1 teaspoon finely grated lemon rind
2 tablespoons lemon juice
2 hard-boiled eggs, quartered

1 Place fish, milk, bay leaf and peppercorns in medium saucepan; bring to the boil. Reduce heat; simmer, uncovered, 10 minutes. Drain; discard liquid and spices. Using disposable kitchen gloves, remove and discard skin from fish; flake flesh into large chunks in medium bowl.
2 Meanwhile, boil, steam or microwave potato until tender; drain. Mash potato with softened butter in large bowl; cover to keep warm.
3 Melt extra butter in medium saucepan; cook onion and garlic, stirring, until onion softens. Add flour; cook, stirring, until mixture thickens and bubbles. Gradually add extra milk; stir until mixture boils and thickens. Add peas, rind and juice; remove from heat. Stir in fish.
4 Preheat grill.
5 Divide egg, fish mixture and potato mixture among four 2-cup (500ml) flameproof dishes. Place dishes on oven tray under very hot grill until tops are browned lightly.
prep + cook time *1 hour 5 minutes*   **serves** *4*
nutritional count per serving *30.2g total fat (19.7g saturated fat); 3160kJ (756 cal); 53.4g carbohydrate; 64g protein; 6.3g fibre*

tuna & cannellini
bean salad

2 cups (400g) dried cannellini beans
425g can tuna in springwater, drained
1 small red onion (100g), sliced thinly
2 trimmed celery stalks (200g), sliced thinly

italian dressing
⅓ cup (80ml) olive oil
⅓ cup (80ml) lemon juice
1 tablespoon finely chopped fresh oregano
2 cloves garlic, crushed

1 Place beans in medium bowl, cover with cold water; stand overnight, drain. Rinse under cold water; drain. Place beans in medium saucepan of boiling water; return to the boil. Reduce heat; simmer, uncovered, about 1 hour or until beans are almost tender. Drain.
2 Meanwhile, make italian dressing.
3 Place beans and dressing in large bowl with tuna, onion and celery; toss gently to combine.
italian dressing Place ingredients in screw-top jar; shake well.

prep + cook time *1 hour 10 minutes (+ standing)*
serves *4*
nutritional count per serving *21.6g total fat (3.8g saturated fat); 1651kJ (395 cal); 17.3g carbohydrate; 28.8g protein; 8.5g fibre*

Oven-baked is the perfect way to make risotto if you're pressed for time – it requires far less attention than the traditional-style risotto, but with equally delicious results.

oven-baked
tuna risotto

3½ cups (875ml) chicken stock
10g butter
2 teaspoons olive oil
1 medium brown onion (150g), chopped finely
1 clove garlic, crushed
1½ cups (300g) arborio rice
425g can tuna in oil, drained
1 cup (120g) frozen peas
250g cherry tomatoes, halved
2 tablespoons lemon juice

1 Preheat oven to 180°C/160°C fan-forced.
2 Bring stock to the boil in medium saucepan.
3 Meanwhile, melt butter with oil in large saucepan; cook onion and garlic, stirring, until onion softens. Add rice; stir to coat in onion mixture. Stir in hot stock and tuna.
4 Place risotto mixture in a large 2.5 litre (10-cup) shallow baking dish; cover with foil. Bake, in oven, 15 minutes, stirring halfway through cooking time. Uncover; bake 20 minutes. Stir in peas, top with tomato; bake, uncovered, about 15 minutes or until rice is tender. Remove from oven, stir in juice.

prep + cook time *1 hour 15 minutes*   serves *4*
nutritional count per serving *25.8g total fat (5.2g saturated fat); 2583kJ (618 cal); 66.3g carbohydrate; 28g protein; 4g fibre*

salmon kedgeree

1½ cups (300g) long-grain white rice
415g can red salmon
80g butter
⅓ cup coarsely chopped fresh flat-leaf parsley
2 teaspoons lemon juice
3 hard-boiled eggs, chopped coarsely

1 Cook rice in large saucepan of boiling water until tender; drain.
2 Drain salmon; discard skin and bones. Flake flesh.
3 Melt butter in large frying pan; add rice, parsley and juice. Cook, stirring, until heated through. Add salmon and eggs; cook, stirring gently, until heated through. Serve with lemon wedges, if you like.

prep + cook time *25 minutes* serves *6*
nutritional count per serving *20.5g total fat (9.9g saturated fat); 1760kJ (421 cal); 39.7g carbohydrate; 19.1g protein; 0.6g fibre*

Homemade salad dressing is not only money-saving, you can add whatever takes your fancy. Use a good-quality olive oil and vinegar – add mustard, freshly ground pepper and salt for extra flavour.

salad niçoise

200g green beans, trimmed
2 tablespoons olive oil
2 tablespoons white wine vinegar
1 tablespoon lemon juice
1 small red onion (100g), sliced thinly
4 medium egg tomatoes (600g), seeded,
  cut into thin wedges
3 hard-boiled eggs, quartered
425g can tuna in spring water, drained, flaked
⅓ cup (40g) seeded small black olives
⅓ cup (55g) rinsed, drained caperberries
2 tablespoons finely shredded fresh basil
1 tablespoon coarsely chopped fresh
  flat-leaf parsley

1 Boil, steam or microwave beans until tender; drain. Rinse under cold water; drain.
2 Whisk oil, vinegar and juice together in large bowl, add beans and remaining ingredients; toss gently to combine.
prep + cook time *20 minutes*   **serves** *4*
nutritional count per serving *15.6g total fat (3.4g saturated fat); 1262kJ (302 cal); 9g carbohydrate; 29.4g protein; 3.9g fibre*

savoury pies & tarts

gruyère, leek & bacon tart

50g butter
2 medium leeks (700g), sliced thinly
2 rindless bacon rashers (130g), chopped finely
2 sheets ready-rolled puff pastry
2 eggs
½ cup (125ml) cream
1 teaspoon fresh thyme leaves
½ cup (60g) finely grated gruyère cheese

1 Preheat oven to 220°C/200°C fan-forced. Oil 24cm-round loose-based flan tin; place tin on oven tray.
2 Melt butter in medium frying pan; cook leek, stirring occasionally, about 15 minutes or until soft. Remove from pan. Cook bacon in same pan, stirring, until crisp; drain on absorbent paper.
3 Meanwhile, place one pastry sheet in flan tin; overlap with second sheet to form cross shape, trim away overlapping pastry. Prick pastry base with fork, cover with baking paper; fill with dried beans or uncooked rice. Bake 20 minutes. Remove paper and beans; cool pastry case.
4 Reduce oven temperature to 200°C/180°C fan-forced.
5 Whisk eggs, cream and thyme in small bowl.
6 Spread leek into pastry case; top with bacon. Pour in egg mixture; sprinkle with cheese. Bake 20 minutes or until filling sets. Cool 10 minutes before serving.
7 Serve tart with a baby rocket and parmesan salad, if you like.

prep + cook time *1 hour 10 minutes* serves *6*
nutritional count per serving *34.8g total fat (20.2g saturated fat); 1948kJ (466 cal); 24.5g carbohydrate; 14.4g protein; 2.8g fibre*

spinach & pumpkin fillo pie

75g butter, melted
1 tablespoon olive oil
1 medium brown onion (150g), chopped finely
2 cloves garlic, crushed
1kg butternut pumpkin, chopped finely
1 tablespoon brown sugar
1 teaspoon ground cumin
½ teaspoon ground nutmeg
2 x 250g frozen spinach, thawed, drained
1 cup (200g) fetta cheese
2 eggs, beaten lightly
6 sheets fillo pastry

1 Brush 24cm ovenproof pie dish with some of the butter.
2 Heat oil in large frying pan; cook onion and garlic, stirring, until onion softens. Add pumpkin, sugar and spices; cook, covered, about 20 minutes or until pumpkin is tender. Stir in spinach and ¾ cup of the cheese. Remove from heat; cool 5 minutes. Stir in egg.
3 Preheat oven to 180°C/160°C fan-forced.
4 Layer two sheets of pastry, brushing each with butter; fold pastry in half widthways, place in pie dish, edges overhanging. Brush pastry with butter again. Repeat with remaining pastry, overlapping the pieces clockwise around the dish. Fold over edges to make a rim around the edge of the pie; brush with remaining butter. Spoon pumpkin mixture into dish.
5 Bake pie about 40 minutes or until browned lightly. Sprinkle with remaining cheese.

prep + cook time *1 hour 20 minutes* serves *6*
nutritional count per serving *24.4g total fat (13.4g saturated fat); 1588kJ (380 cal); 23.2g carbohydrate; 15g protein; 5.1g fibre*

We've added pumpkin to the spinach to give a new look to the traditional Greek recipe for spanakopita. You could also make this pie in individual pie dishes.

creamy fish pie

10g butter
2 teaspoons olive oil
1 small brown onion (80g), chopped finely
1 medium carrot (120g), chopped finely
1 trimmed celery stalk (100g), chopped finely
1 tablespoon plain flour
1 cup (250ml) fish stock
500g firm white fish fillets, chopped coarsely
½ cup (125ml) cream
1 tablespoon english mustard
1 cup (120g) frozen peas
½ cup (40g) finely grated parmesan cheese
1 sheet ready-rolled puff pastry
1 egg, beaten lightly

1 Preheat oven to 220°C/200°C fan-forced.
2 Melt butter with oil in large saucepan; cook onion, carrot and celery, stirring, until carrot softens. Stir in flour; cook, stirring, 2 minutes. Add stock and fish; cook, stirring, until fish is cooked through and mixture boils and thickens. Remove from heat; stir in cream, mustard, peas and cheese.
3 Spoon mixture into a shallow small 1.5 litre (6-cup) baking dish; top with pastry. Brush top with egg. Bake about 20 minutes or until browned.

prep + cook time *1 hour*   serves *4*
nutritional count per serving *35.1g total fat (19.1g saturated fat); 2366kJ (566 cal); 23.5g carbohydrate; 37.5g protein; 4.1g fibre*

You can stir ¼ cup coarsely chopped fresh flat-leaf parsley into the mixture when adding the fish. It is important you use a shallow baking dish so that the top of the fish mixture is touching the pastry and the pastry is not stuck to the sides of the dish, as this could prevent it from rising. You can use any firm white fish fillet you like, such as blue-eye, ling or snapper, in this recipe.

egg & cheese tartlets
with capsicum relish

Balsamic white vinegar is a clear and lighter version of balsamic vinegar; it has a fresh, sweet clean taste, and is available from major supermarkets and good delicatessens.

2 sheets ready-rolled puff pastry
2 teaspoons olive oil
2 shallots (50g), sliced thinly
4 eggs
¼ cup (60ml) cream
½ cup (40g) finely grated parmesan cheese
30g baby rocket leaves

capsicum relish
1 tablespoon olive oil
1 small red onion (100g), sliced thinly
2 medium red capsicum (400g), sliced thinly
⅓ cup (80ml) white balsamic vinegar
2 tablespoons brown sugar
½ cup (125ml) water

1 Preheat oven to 220°C/200°C fan-forced. Oil a six-hole (¾-cup/180ml) texas muffin pan.
2 Cut pastry sheets in half; cut halves into three rectangles. Overlap two rectangles to form cross shapes; push gently into pan holes to cover bases and sides. Prick bases with fork, cover with baking paper; fill with dried beans or uncooked rice.
3 Bake pastry cases 10 minutes. Remove paper and beans carefully from pan holes; bake about 5 minutes or until browned lightly. Cool pastry cases in pan. Reduce oven temperature to 200°C/180°C fan-forced.
4 Meanwhile, make capsicum relish.
5 Heat oil in small frying pan. Add shallot; cook until soft.
6 Whisk eggs and cream in medium bowl; mix in cheese and shallots. Fill pastry cases with egg mixture. Bake about 15 minutes or until set.
7 Serve tartlets with relish and rocket.
capsicum relish Heat oil in large frying pan. Add onion and capsicum; cook about 10 minutes or until vegetables are soft. Add vinegar, sugar and the water; cook, stirring occasionally, about 15 minutes or until mixture thickens slightly.

prep + cook time *50 minutes (+ cooling)* serves *6* nutritional count per serving *27.3g total fat (12.7g saturated fat); 1697kJ (406 cal); 28g carbohydrate; 11.7g protein; 1.7g fibre*

beef & onion party pies

1 tablespoon vegetable oil
1 medium brown onion (150g), chopped finely
450g beef mince
2 tablespoons tomato paste
2 tablespoons worcestershire sauce
2 tablespoons powdered gravy mix
¾ cup (180ml) water
3 sheets ready-rolled shortcrust pastry
1 egg, beaten lightly
2 sheets ready-rolled puff pastry

1 Heat oil in large frying pan; cook onion, stirring, until onion softens. Add beef; cook, stirring, until beef changes colour. Add paste, sauce, and blended gravy powder and the water; bring to the boil, stirring. Reduce heat; simmer, uncovered, about 10 minutes or until thickened slightly; cool.
2 Preheat oven to 200°C/180°C fan-forced. Oil two 12-hole (2-tablespoons/40ml) deep flat-based patty pans.
3 Cut twenty-four 7cm rounds from shortcrust pastry; press into pan holes. Divide beef mixture among pastry cases. Brush edges with a little of the egg.
4 Cut twenty-four 6cm rounds from puff pastry; top pies with puff pastry lids. Press edges firmly to seal; brush lids with remaining egg. Cut a small slit in top of each pie.
5 Bake pies about 20 minutes or until browned lightly. Stand pies in pan 5 minutes before serving.
prep + cook time *1 hour* makes *24*
nutritional count per pie *11.2g total fat (5.4g saturated fat); 790kJ (189 cal); 15.5g carbohydrate; 6.4g protein; 0.7g fibre*

fetta & spinach fillo bundles

350g spinach, trimmed
1 tablespoon olive oil
1 medium brown onion (150g), chopped finely
2 cloves garlic, crushed
½ teaspoon ground nutmeg
150g fetta cheese, crumbled
3 eggs
2 teaspoons finely grated lemon rind
¼ cup coarsely chopped fresh mint
2 tablespoons finely chopped fresh dill
80g butter, melted
6 sheets fillo pastry

1 Boil, steam or microwave spinach until wilted; drain. Refresh in cold water; drain. Squeeze out excess moisture. Chop spinach coarsely; spread out on absorbent paper.
2 Heat oil in small frying pan; cook onion and garlic, stirring, until onion softens. Add nutmeg; cook, stirring, until fragrant. Cool.
3 Combine onion mixture and spinach in medium bowl with cheese, eggs, rind and herbs.
4 Preheat oven to 200°C/180°C fan-forced. Brush six-hole (¾-cup/180ml) texas muffin pan with a little of the butter.
5 Brush each sheet of fillo with melted butter; fold in half to enclose buttered side. Gently press one sheet into each pan hole.
6 Divide spinach mixture among pastry cases; fold fillo over filling to enclose. Brush with butter. Bake 15 minutes. Turn fillo bundles out, top-side up, onto baking-paper-lined oven tray; bake 5 minutes or until browned. Stand 5 minutes before serving, top-side up.
prep + cook time *45 minutes*   **makes 6**
nutritional count per bundle *22.9g total fat (12.3g saturated fat); 1200kJ (287 cal); 9.6g carbohydrate; 10.4g protein; 1.8g fibre*

quiche lorraine

1 medium brown onion (150g), chopped finely
3 rindless bacon rashers (195g), chopped finely
3 eggs
300ml cream
½ cup (125ml) milk
¾ cup (120g) coarsely grated gruyère cheese

pastry
1¾ cups (260g) plain flour
150g cold butter, chopped coarsely
1 egg yolk
2 teaspoons lemon juice
⅓ cup (80ml) iced water, approximately

1 Make pastry.
2 Preheat oven to 200°C/180°C fan-forced.
3 Roll pastry between sheets of baking paper large enough to line a deep 23cm loose-based flan tin. Lift pastry into tin; gently press pastry around side. Trim edge, place tin on oven tray. Cover pastry with baking paper; fill with dried beans or rice. Bake 10 minutes; remove paper and beans. Bake pastry about 10 minutes or until golden brown; cool.
4 Reduce oven temperature to 180°C/160°C fan-forced.
5 Cook onion and bacon in heated oiled small frying pan until onion is soft; drain on absorbent paper, cool. Sprinkle bacon mixture over pastry case.
6 Whisk eggs in medium bowl then whisk in cream, milk and cheese; pour into pastry case. Bake about 35 minutes or until filling is set. Stand quiche 5 minutes before removing quiche from tin.
pastry Sift flour into bowl; rub in butter. Add egg yolk, juice and enough water to make ingredients cling together. Knead gently on lightly floured surface until smooth; cover, refrigerate 30 minutes.
prep + cook time *1 hour 30 minutes (+ refrigeration)* **serves** *6*
nutritional count per serving *58.1g total fat (35.4g saturated fat); 3139kJ (751 cal); 35.4g carbohydrate; 22.1g protein; 2g fibre*

moroccan tart

You can top this tart with finely chopped fresh flat-leaf parsley or mint leaves and serve with a salad of baby spinach and orange segments, if you like.

1 sheet ready-rolled shortcrust pastry, thawed
1 tablespoon olive oil
300g lamb mince
1 teaspoon ground coriander
½ teaspoon ground cinnamon
400g can chickpeas, rinsed, drained
1 clove garlic, crushed
2 tablespoons lemon juice
1 piece preserved lemon (35g), trimmed, chopped finely
2 tablespoons roasted pine nuts
125g fetta cheese, crumbled

1 Preheat oven to 200°C/180°C fan-forced.
2 Roll pastry out to 28cm x 30cm rectangle; place on oiled oven tray. Fold edges of pastry over to make a 1cm border all the way around pastry. Prick pastry base with fork; bake 10 minutes.
3 Meanwhile, heat half the oil in medium frying pan; cook lamb, coriander and cinnamon, stirring, 5 minutes. Drain away excess oil.
4 Combine chickpeas, garlic, juice and remaining oil in medium bowl. Using fork, coarsely mash mixture; stir in preserved lemon. Spread over pastry base. Top with lamb mixture; sprinkle with nuts and cheese. Bake about 10 minutes.

prep + cook time *45 minutes* **serves** *4*
nutritional count per serving *34.8g total fat (14.3g saturated fat); 2274kJ (544 cal); 27.7g carbohydrate; 28.4g protein; 4.4g fibre*

fish chowder pies

40g butter
1 medium brown onion (150g), chopped coarsely
1 clove garlic, crushed
3 rindless bacon rashers (195g), chopped coarsely
2 tablespoons plain flour
1 cup (250ml) milk
½ cup (125ml) cream
2 small potatoes (240g), cut into 1cm pieces
600g firm white fish fillets, cut into 2cm pieces
¼ cup finely chopped fresh chives
2 sheets ready-rolled shortcrust pastry
1 egg, beaten lightly
2 sheets ready-rolled puff pastry

1 Melt butter in large saucepan; cook onion, garlic and bacon, stirring, until onion softens.
2 Add flour; cook, stirring, 1 minute. Gradually stir in combined milk and cream; bring to the boil. Add potato; simmer, covered, stirring occasionally, 8 minutes. Add fish; simmer, uncovered, 2 minutes; cool. Stir in chives.
3 Preheat oven to 200°C/180°C fan-forced. Grease six-hole (¾-cup/180ml) texas muffin pan.
4 Cut six 12cm rounds from shortcrust pastry; press into pan holes. Brush edges with a little of the egg. Divide fish chowder among pastry cases.
5 Cut six 9cm rounds from puff pastry; top chowder with puff pastry rounds. Press edges firmly to seal; brush tops with remaining egg. Cut a small slit in top of each pie.
6 Bake pies about 25 minutes. Stand pies in pan 5 minutes before serving, top-side up, sprinkled with chopped fresh chives.

prep + cook time 1 hour 5 minutes makes 6
nutritional count per pie 49.8g total fat
(27.4g saturated fat); 3415kJ (817 cal); 55.9g
carbohydrate; 35.5g protein; 2.9g fibre

Lamb leftovers can be chopped or diced and used in a dish such as this shepherd's pie, or used as a base for a curry.

shepherd's pie

30g butter
1 medium brown onion (150g), chopped finely
1 medium carrot (120g), chopped finely
½ teaspoon dried mixed herbs
4 cups (750g) finely chopped cooked lamb
¼ cup (70g) tomato paste
¼ cup (60ml) tomato sauce
2 tablespoons worcestershire sauce
2 cups (500ml) beef stock
2 tablespoons plain flour
⅓ cup (80ml) water

potato topping
5 medium potatoes (1kg), cut in chunks
60g butter
¼ cup (60ml) milk

1 Preheat oven to 200°C/180°C fan-forced. Oil shallow 2.5-litre (10 cup) ovenproof dish.
2 Make potato topping.
3 Meanwhile, heat butter in large saucepan; cook onion and carrot, stirring, until tender. Add mixed herbs and lamb; cook, stirring, 2 minutes. Stir in paste, sauces and stock, then blended flour and water; stir over heat until mixture boils and thickens. Pour mixture into dish.
4 Drop heaped tablespoons of potato topping onto lamb mixture. Bake in oven about 20 minutes or until browned and heated through.
potato topping Boil, steam or microwave potato until tender; drain. Mash with butter and milk until smooth.

prep + cook time *1 hour* serves *4*
nutritional count per serving *36.2g total fat (20.2g saturated fat); 2976kJ (712 cal); 44.7g carbohydrate; 48.8g protein; 6g fibre*

caramelised onion tarts

40g butter
1 tablespoon olive oil
3 large brown onions (600g), sliced thinly
2 tablespoons brown sugar
2 tablespoons balsamic vinegar
½ cup (125ml) water
2 sheets ready-rolled puff pastry
¼ cup (60g) ricotta cheese

1 Oil 4 x 12cm loose-based flan tins.
2 Melt butter with oil in large frying pan, add onion, sugar and vinegar; cook, stirring, until very soft and browned lightly. Add the water; cook, stirring, until water has evaporated.
3 Meanwhile, cut pastry sheets in half diagonally. Line tins with pastry, press into sides; trim edges, prick bases with fork. Freeze 15 minutes.
4 Preheat oven to 220°C/200°C fan-forced.
5 Place tins on oven tray; bake 15 minutes.
6 Top tarts with caramelised onion, gently push onion down to flatten pastry; sprinkle with cheese. Bake about 5 minutes.

prep + cook time *1 hour 10 minutes (+ freezing)*
serves *4*
nutritional count per serving *33.5g total fat (17.3g saturated fat); 2161kJ (517 cal); 44.6g carbohydrate; 8.4g protein; 3.1g fibre*

You could also make this as one large tart. These tarts are not baked with baking weights so the pastry will puff up. Gently push the pastry down when topping it with the onion. If you have some, sprinkle 1 tablespoon of fresh thyme leaves over tarts just before serving.

spinach & beetroot tart

1 sheet ready-rolled puff pasty
250g frozen spinach, thawed, drained
1 cup (200g) fetta cheese, crumbled
½ x 850g can drained baby beetroot, sliced thinly

1 Preheat oven to 220°C/200°C fan-forced.
2 Place pastry on an oiled oven tray. Fold edges of
pastry over to make a 0.5cm border all the way
around pastry. Prick pastry base with fork. Place
another oven tray on top of pastry; bake 10 minutes.
Remove top tray from pastry; reduce oven
temperature to 200°C/180°C fan-forced.
3 Meanwhile, combine spinach with half the cheese
in medium bowl.
4 Top tart with spinach mixture, beetroot and
remaining cheese. Bake about 10 minutes.
prep + cook time *50 minutes (+ freezing)* **serves 4**
nutritional count per serving *21.4g total fat
(12.8g saturated fat); 1421kJ (340 cal); 22.1g
carbohydrate; 13.4g protein; 4g fibre*

Drain the spinach very thoroughly so that the
moisture does not seep into the tart base and
make the pastry soggy.

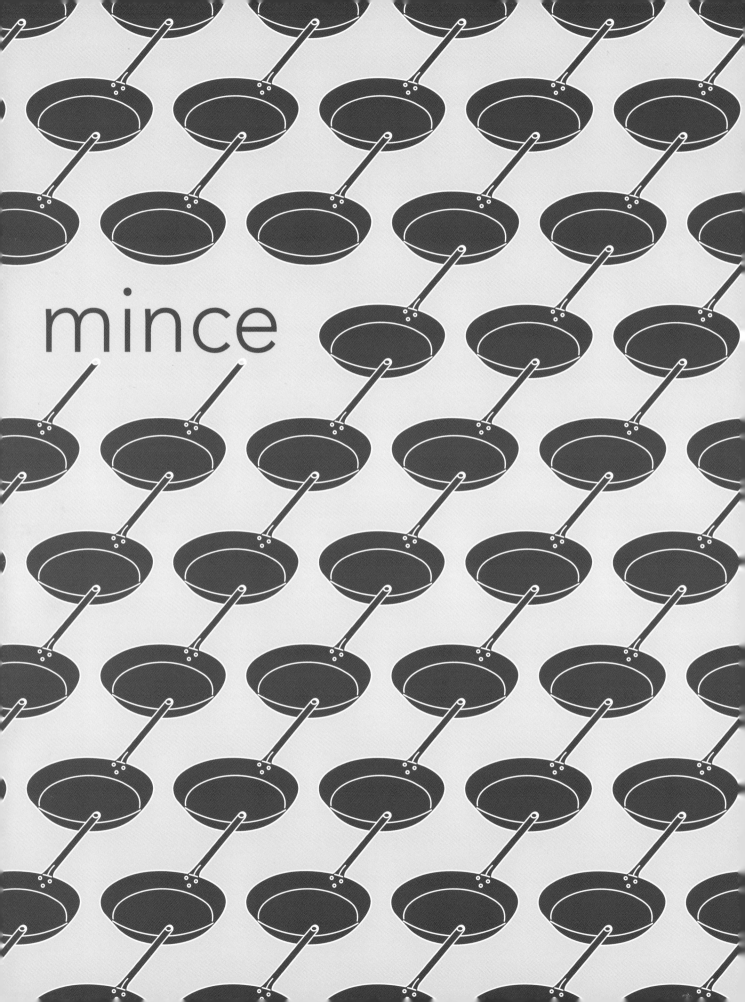

mince

cheeseburgers with caramelised onion

500g beef mince
4 thin slices (40g) cheddar cheese
4 hamburger buns, split
1 small tomato (90g), sliced thinly
8 large butter lettuce leaves
4 large dill pickles (240g), sliced thinly
1 tablespoon american-style mustard
⅓ cup (95g) tomato sauce

caramelised onion
2 tablespoons olive oil
2 medium white onions (300g), sliced thinly
1 tablespoon brown sugar
2 tablespoons balsamic vinegar
2 tablespoons water

1 Make caramelised onion.
2 Shape mince into 4 patties; cook on heated oiled grill plate (or grill or barbecue) until cooked through. Top each patty with cheese slices during last minute of cooking time.
3 Meanwhile, toast buns, cut-sides down, on same grill plate.
4 Place cheeseburgers, onion, tomato, lettuce and pickle between toasted buns; serve with mustard and tomato sauce.

caramelised onion Heat oil in large frying pan; cook onion, stirring, until soft. Add sugar, vinegar and the water; cook, stirring, until onion is caramelised.

prep + cook time **55 minutes** serves **4**
nutritional count per serving **23.6g total fat (7.4g saturated fat); 2378kJ (569 cal); 51.6g carbohydrate; 34.9g protein; 5g fibre**

moussaka

¼ cup (60ml) olive oil
2 large eggplants (1kg), sliced thinly
1 large brown onion (200g), chopped finely
2 cloves garlic, crushed
1kg lamb mince
425g can crushed tomatoes
½ cup (125ml) dry white wine
1 teaspoon ground cinnamon
¼ cup (20g) finely grated parmesan cheese

white sauce
80g butter
⅓ cup (50g) plain flour
2 cups (500ml) milk

1 Heat oil in large frying pan; cook eggplant, in batches, until browned both sides; drain on absorbent paper.
2 Cook onion and garlic in same pan, stirring, until onion softens. Add mince; cook, stirring, until mince changes colour. Stir in undrained tomatoes, wine and cinnamon; bring to the boil. Reduce heat; simmer, uncovered, about 30 minutes or until liquid has evaporated.
3 Meanwhile, preheat oven to 180°C/160°C fan-forced. Oil shallow 2-litre (8-cup) rectangular baking dish.
4 Make white sauce.
5 Place a third of the eggplant, overlapping slices slightly, in dish; spread half of the meat sauce over eggplant. Repeat layering with another third of the eggplant, remaining meat sauce and remaining eggplant. Spread white sauce over top layer; sprinkle with cheese.
6 Bake moussaka about 40 minutes or until top browns lightly. Cover; stand 10 minutes before serving. Serve with a green salad, if you like.
white sauce Melt butter in medium saucepan, add flour; cook, stirring, until mixture bubbles and thickens. Gradually add milk; stir until mixture boils and thickens.
prep + cook time *1 hour 50 minutes* **serves** *6*
nutritional count per serving *36.6g total fat (16.5g saturated fat); 2420kJ (579 cal); 18g carbohydrate; 41.8g protein; 5.3g fibre*

Look out for specials on minced beef when planning to cook rissoles or a bolognese sauce. Buy in bulk and freeze in half-kilo plastic bags.

rissoles with cabbage mash

Rissoles can be prepared a day ahead; refrigerate, covered, until required.

2 rindless bacon rashers (130g), chopped finely
1 small brown onion (80g), chopped finely
1 clove garlic, crushed
1 fresh red thai chilli, chopped finely
1 tablespoon worcestershire sauce
1 cup (70g) stale breadcrumbs
1 egg
¼ cup coarsely chopped fresh flat-leaf parsley
500g beef mince
2 tablespoons barbecue sauce
1 tablespoon vegetable oil
1 tablespoon dijon mustard
2 cups (500ml) beef stock
1 tablespoon cornflour
2 tablespoons water

cabbage mash
1kg potatoes, quartered
¼ cup (60ml) cream
30g butter, chopped
200g finely shredded savoy cabbage
1 small white onion (80g), chopped finely

1 Cook potato for cabbage mash.
2 Cook bacon, onion, garlic and chilli in medium frying pan, stirring until onion softens. Remove from heat.
3 Using hands, combine worcestershire sauce, breadcrumbs, egg, parsley, mince and half of the barbecue sauce with bacon mixture in large bowl; shape mixture into eight rissoles.
4 Heat oil in same pan; cook rissoles, in batches, until browned both sides and cooked through. Cover to keep warm.
5 Place mustard, stock and remaining barbecue sauce in same pan; bring to the boil. Stir in blended cornflour and water; cook, stirring, until gravy boils and thickens slightly.
6 Finish cabbage mash. Serve rissoles with cabbage mash and topped with gravy.
cabbage mash Boil, steam or microwave potato until tender; drain. Mash potato with cream and butter until smooth; stir in cabbage and onion.
prep + cook time *45 minutes* **serves 4**
nutritional count per serving *33.2g total fat (14.9g saturated fat); 2959kJ (708 cal); 53.5g carbohydrate; 45.2g protein; 7.1g fibre*

warm split pea
& sausage salad

1½ cups (300g) yellow split peas
2 rindless bacon rashers (130g), chopped coarsely
6 thin sausages (480g), chopped coarsely
1 medium carrot (120g), chopped coarsely
1 trimmed celery stalk (100g), chopped coarsely
1 medium brown onion (150g), chopped coarsely
2 cloves garlic, sliced thinly
250g grape tomatoes, halved
400g can white beans, rinsed, drained
2 teaspoons finely grated orange rind
⅓ cup (80ml) orange juice

1 Place peas in medium bowl, cover with cold water; stand overnight. Drain peas, rinse under cold water; drain again.
2 Place peas in medium saucepan, cover with boiling water. Simmer, covered, about 10 minutes or until peas are tender; rinse under cold water, drain.
3 Meanwhile, cook bacon and sausage in large heated saucepan, in batches, until sausage is cooked.
4 Add carrot, celery, onion and garlic to pan; cook, stirring, until carrot softens slightly. Add tomatoes; cook, stirring, 2 minutes. Add beans, peas, bacon and sausage; stir to combine. Remove from heat; stir in rind and juice.

prep + cook time **40 minutes (+ standing)** serves **4**
nutritional count per serving **33.9g total fat (15.1g saturated fat); 2985kJ (714 cal); 51.2g carbohydrate; 43g protein; 16.8g fibre**

We used thin lamb merguez sausages. If you have some, stir ⅓ cup coarsely chopped fresh flat-leaf parsley into this recipe.

meatloaf with
stir-fried cabbage

700g beef mince
2 cloves garlic, crushed
1 small brown onion (80g), chopped finely
1 small carrot (70g), grated coarsely
⅓ cup (35g) packaged breadcrumbs
1 egg
4cm piece fresh ginger (20g), chopped finely
2 tablespoons light soy sauce
¼ cup (60ml) hoisin sauce
1 tablespoon peanut oil
4 cups (320g) finely sliced cabbage
1 teaspoon sesame oil

1 Preheat oven to 180°C/160°C fan-forced.
2 Combine mince, garlic, onion, carrot, breadcrumbs, egg, half the ginger, half the soy sauce and 2 tablespoons of the hoisin sauce in large bowl. Press mixture firmly into oiled 14cm x 21cm loaf pan; bake, uncovered, about 45 minutes or until meatloaf shrinks from the sides of the pan.
3 Meanwhile, heat peanut oil in wok; stir-fry remaining ginger. Add cabbage; stir-fry until wilted. Remove from heat; stir in sesame oil.
4 Slice meatloaf; drizzle with combined remaining sauces. Serve with stir-fried cabbage.

prep + cook time *1 hour* serves **4**
nutritional count per serving *20.5g total fat (6.7g saturated fat); 1777kJ (425 cal); 16.4g carbohydrate; 40.9g protein; 6.1g fibre*

You need approximately a third of a small savoy cabbage for this recipe. If you don't have cabbage, stir-fry any vegetable that takes your fancy – buk choy and gai lan stir-fry particularly well.

beef enchiladas

2 tablespoons olive oil

1 small yellow capsicum (150g), chopped finely

1 small red onion (100g), chopped finely

1 clove garlic, crushed

1 teaspoon ground cumin

½ teaspoon sweet paprika

400g beef mince

2 tablespoons tomato paste

2 tablespoons water

130g can kidney beans, rinsed, drained

2 tablespoons coarsely chopped fresh oregano

2 cups (500ml) bottled tomato pasta sauce

1 cup (250ml) water, extra

10 x 15cm corn tortillas

1 cup (120g) coarsely grated reduced-fat
    cheddar cheese

1 tablespoon finely chopped fresh
    flat-leaf parsley

1 Heat half the oil in large frying pan; cook capsicum, half the onion and half the garlic, stirring, until vegetables soften. Add spices; cook, stirring, until fragrant. Add mince; cook, stirring, until changed in colour. Stir in paste and the 2 tablespoons water; simmer, stirring, 1 minute. Place filling mixture in large heatproof bowl; stir in beans and oregano.

2 Heat remaining oil in same pan; cook remaining onion and garlic, stirring, until onion softens. Add pasta sauce and the extra water; bring to the boil. Reduce heat; simmer, uncovered, 5 minutes.

3 Preheat oven to 180°C/160°C fan-forced. Oil shallow square 3-litre (12-cup) ovenproof dish. Spread ½ cup pasta sauce mixture in dish.

4 Warm tortillas according to package instructions. Dip tortillas, one at a time, in pasta sauce mixture; place on board. Divide filling among tortillas, placing mixture on edge of tortilla; roll tortillas to enclose filling.

5 Place enchiladas, seam-side down, snugly in single layer, in dish. Spread remaining pasta sauce mixture over enchiladas; sprinkle with cheese. Cook, uncovered, about 15 minutes or until enchiladas are hot.

6 Serve enchiladas sprinkled with parsley and, if you like, separate small bowls of sour cream, shredded lettuce and chopped tomatoes.

prep + cook time *1 hour 15 minutes*   serves *4*
nutritional count per serving *26.7g total fat (9.2g saturated fat); 2696kJ (645 cal); 57.4g carbohydrate; 38.8g protein; 10.1g fibre*

meat pies

1½ cups (225g) plain flour
100g cold butter, chopped coarsely
1 egg
1 tablespoon iced water, approximately
2 sheets ready-rolled puff pastry
1 egg, extra

beef filling
1 tablespoon vegetable oil
1 small brown onion (80g), chopped finely
600g beef mince
415g can crushed tomatoes
2 tablespoons tomato paste
2 tablespoons worcestershire sauce
¾ cup (180ml) beef stock

1 Process flour and butter until crumbly. Add egg and enough of the water to make ingredients cling together. Knead pastry on lightly floured surface until smooth. Cover; refrigerate 30 minutes.
2 Meanwhile, make beef filling.
3 Oil six ⅔-cup (160ml) pie tins. Divide pastry into six portions; roll each between sheets of baking paper until large enough to line tins. Lift pastry into tins; gently press over base and sides; trim. Refrigerate 30 minutes.
4 Cut six 11cm rounds from puff pastry. Refrigerate until required.
5 Preheat oven to 200°C/180°C fan-forced.
6 Place pastry cases on oven tray; line pastry with baking paper then fill with dried beans or uncooked rice. Bake 10 minutes; remove paper and beans. Bake 5 minutes. Cool.
7 Fill pastry cases with beef filling; brush edges of pastry with extra egg. Top with puff pastry rounds; press edges to seal. Brush tops with egg. Cut steam holes in pies. Bake about 20 minutes. Serve pies with tomato sauce, if you like.
beef filling Heat oil in large saucepan, add onion and beef; cook, stirring, until beef is well browned. Stir in undrained crushed tomatoes, paste, sauce and stock; bring to the boil. Reduce heat, simmer, uncovered, about 20 minutes or until thick. Cool.
prep + cook time *1 hour 35 minutes (+ refrigeration)* **makes** *6*
nutritional count per pie *38.7g total fat (13.8g saturated fat); 2876kJ (688 cal); 52.4g carbohydrate; 31.2g protein; 3.5g fibre*

rissole, bacon &
tomato casserole

600g beef mince
1 small brown onion (80g), chopped finely
1 egg
½ cup (100g) white long-grain rice
¼ cup (15g) stale breadcrumbs
2 teaspoons worcestershire sauce
4 bacon rashers (280g), chopped finely
400g can diced tomatoes
½ cup (125ml) beef stock
2 tablespoon tomato paste
½ cup coarsely chopped fresh basil

1 Preheat oven to 200°C/180°C fan-forced.
2 Combine mince, onion, egg, rice, breadcrumbs and sauce in large bowl. Shape mixture into 12 rissoles; place into deep 2-litre (8-cup) ovenproof dish.
3 Sprinkle bacon over rissoles; pour over combined tomatoes, stock and paste.
4 Bake casserole, covered, 1 hour or until rissoles are cooked through and rice is tender. Stir in basil before serving.
prep + cook time *1 hour 15 minutes*   **serves** *4*
nutritional count per serving *27.4g total fat (11g saturated fat); 2353kJ (563 cal); 28.8g carbohydrate; 49.1g protein; 2.4g fibre*

rissoles with
grilled onions

2 rindless bacon rashers (130g), chopped finely
1 small brown onion (80g), chopped finely
500g beef mince
1 cup (70g) stale breadcrumbs
1 egg
2 tablespoons barbecue sauce
1 tablespoon worcestershire sauce
1 tablespoon olive oil
3 medium brown onions (450g), sliced thinly
2 tablespoons brown sugar
1 tablespoon malt vinegar

1 Cook bacon and onion in oiled medium frying pan, stirring, until onion softens. Cool.
2 Combine mince, breadcrumbs, egg, sauces and bacon mixture in large bowl; shape mixture into 12 rissoles.
3 Cook rissoles on heated barbecue grill plate until cooked as desired.
4 Meanwhile, heat oil on barbecue flat plate; cook onions, stirring, until browned lightly. Add sugar and vinegar; cook, stirring, about 5 minutes or until onions caramelise.
5 Serve rissoles with grilled onions and, if you like, a mixed green salad.

prep + cook time *40 minutes* serves *4*
nutritional count per serving *19.9g total fat
(6.5g saturated fat); 1944kJ (465 cal); 31.7g
carbohydrate; 38.3g protein; 3.7g fibre*

pork cabbage rolls

18 large cabbage leaves
½ cup (100g) uncooked white long-grain rice
250g pork mince
1 medium brown onion (150g), chopped finely
¼ cup finely chopped fresh dill
1 clove garlic, crushed
1 tablespoon tomato paste
2 teaspoons ground cumin
1 teaspoon ground coriander
1 teaspoon ground allspice
4 cloves garlic, quartered
2 medium tomatoes (300g), chopped coarsely
2 x 400g cans crushed tomatoes
¼ cup (60ml) lemon juice

1 Discard thick stems from 15 cabbage leaves; reserve remaining leaves. Boil, steam or microwave trimmed leaves until just pliable; drain. Rinse under cold water; drain. Pat dry with absorbent paper.
2 Using hand, combine rice, pork, onion, dill, crushed garlic, paste and spices in medium bowl.
3 Place one trimmed leaf, vein-side up, on board; cut leaf in half lengthways. Place 1 rounded teaspoon of the pork mixture at stem end of each half; roll each half firmly to enclose filling. Repeat with remaining trimmed leaves.
4 Place reserved leaves in base of large saucepan. Place only enough rolls, seam-side down, in single layer, to completely cover leaves in base of saucepan. Top with quartered garlic, chopped fresh tomato then remaining rolls.
5 Pour undrained tomatoes and juice over cabbage rolls; bring to the boil. Reduce heat; simmer, covered, 1 hour. Uncover; simmer about 30 minutes or until cabbage rolls are cooked through.
6 Serve with thick greek-style yogurt flavoured with a little finely choppped preserved lemon, if you like.
prep + cook time *2 hours 40 minutes*   serves *6*
nutritional count per serving *3.6g total fat (1.1g saturated fat); 803kJ (192 cal); 24.7g carbohydrate; 14.3g protein; 9.7g fibre*

gourmet beef burgers

750g beef mince
1 cup (70g) stale breadcrumbs
2 tablespoons finely chopped fresh flat-leaf parsley
2 tablespoons sun-dried tomato paste
125g mozzarella cheese, sliced thinly
½ cup (150g) mayonnaise
4 bread rolls
50g mesclun
1 small red onion (100g), sliced thinly
2 tablespoons drained, sliced sun-dried
   tomatoes in oil

1 Combine mince, breadcrumbs, parsley and 1½ tablespoons of the paste in large bowl. Shape mixture into four patties.
2 Cook patties on heated oiled grill plate (or grill or barbecue) until browned and cooked through. Top patties with cheese; cook until cheese melts.
3 Combine remaining paste and mayonnaise in small bowl.
4 Split rolls in half. Place each half cut-side down onto grill plate; cook until lightly toasted.
5 Sandwich patties, mayonnaise mixture, mesclun, onion and sliced tomatoes between bread rolls.
prep + cook time 25 minutes   **serves** 4
nutritional count per serving 35g total fat (11.6g saturated fat); 3119kJ (746 cal); 50.4g carbohydrate; 55g protein; 4.7g fibre

When making burgers, buy extra mince — make more patties than you need and freeze them in a sealed container for next time.

oven-baked risotto
with italian sausages

500g spicy italian-style sausages
4 cups (1 litre) chicken stock
1 tablespoon olive oil
40g butter
2 large brown onions (400g), chopped coarsely
1 clove garlic, crushed
2 cups (400g) arborio rice
¾ cup (180ml) dry white wine
1 cup (160g) drained semi-dried tomatoes
¼ cup fresh basil leaves
¼ cup (20g) coarsely grated parmesan cheese

1 Preheat oven to 180°C/160°C fan-forced.
2 Heat flameproof dish on stove top; add sausages and cook until browned all over and cooked through. Remove from dish; slice thickly.
3 Meanwhile, add stock to medium saucepan; bring to the boil.
4 Heat oil and butter in same flameproof dish; cook onion and garlic, stirring, until soft. Add rice; stir to coat in the onion mixture. Add wine, bring to the boil then simmer, uncovered, 1 minute. Add stock, sausages and tomatoes; cover with lid and bake about 25 minutes or until liquid is absorbed and rice is tender. Stir once during cooking.
5 Stir in the basil and cheese.

prep + cook time **55 minutes**   serves **6**
nutritional count per serving   **36.8g total fat (14.4g saturated fat); 3114kJ (745 cal); 68.6g carbohydrate; 27.6g protein; 5.5g fibre**

This recipe showcases the significant influences on Singaporean cooking taken from the cuisines of its near neighbours. Borrowing culinary techniques from Malaysia, India and China, chillies and spices laced with coconut milk are a characteristic of this island nation's cuisine.

meatballs in spicy
coconut milk

800g beef mince

2 eggs

2 teaspoons cornflour

2 cloves garlic, crushed

1 tablespoon finely chopped fresh coriander

1 fresh long red chilli, chopped finely

2 purple shallots (50g), chopped coarsely

3 cloves garlic, quartered

1 teaspoon chilli flakes

7 fresh long red chillies, chopped coarsely

2 tablespoons peanut oil

2cm piece fresh galangal (10g), sliced thinly

3 large tomatoes (660g), seeded, chopped coarsely

400ml can coconut milk

1 tablespoon kecap asin

1 large tomato (220g), seeded, diced

½ cup (40g) fried shallots

1 fresh small red chilli, sliced thinly

1 Combine mince, eggs, cornflour, crushed garlic, coriander and finely chopped chilli in medium bowl; roll level tablespoons of mixture into balls. Place meatballs, in single layer, in large baking-paper-lined bamboo steamer. Steam, covered, over wok of simmering water 10 minutes.

2 Meanwhile, blend or process purple shallots, quartered garlic, chilli flakes, coarsely chopped chilli and half of the oil until mixture forms a paste.

3 Heat remaining oil in wok; cook shallot paste and galangal, stirring, about 1 minute or until fragrant. Add chopped tomato; cook, stirring, 1 minute. Add coconut milk, kecap asin and meatballs; simmer, uncovered, stirring occasionally, about 5 minutes or until meatballs are cooked through and sauce thickens slightly.

4 Serve curry topped with diced tomato, fried shallots and thinly sliced chilli.

prep + cook time **45 minutes**   serves **4**
nutritional count per serving **47.1g total fat (26.5g saturated fat); 2721kJ (651 cal); 8.3g carbohydrate; 47.7g protein; 3.9g fibre**

When making fresh breadcrumbs, freeze in user-friendly portions – they're incredibly useful to have on hand

burgers italian-style

You can use roasted capsicum, available in jars from supermarkets and delicatessens, instead of roasting your own, if you like.

750g beef mince
1 medium red onion (170g), chopped finely
1¼ cups (85g) stale breadcrumbs
1 egg
½ cup (40g) finely grated parmesan cheese
⅓ cup finely chopped fresh flat-leaf parsley
1 clove garlic, crushed
1 teaspoon chilli flakes
3 medium red capsicums (600g)
1 tablespoon olive oil
12 slices ciabatta bread (420g)
150g drained marinated artichoke hearts,
    sliced thinly
60g rocket leaves

ripe tomato sauce
1 tablespoon olive oil
3 cloves garlic, sliced thinly
500g ripe small tomatoes, sliced thickly
2 teaspoons balsamic vinegar

1 Make ripe tomato sauce.
2 Meanwhile, combine mince, onion, breadcrumbs, egg, cheese, parsley, garlic and chilli flakes in medium bowl; shape mixture into six patties. Place patties on tray, cover; refrigerate until required.
3 Quarter capsicums; discard seeds and membranes. Roast under preheated grill or in very hot oven, skin-side up, until skin blisters and blackens. Cover capsicum pieces with plastic or paper for 5 minutes; peel away skin then slice capsicum thinly.
4 Heat oil in large frying pan; cook patties about 5 minutes each side or until cooked through.
5 Preheat grill.
6 Place bread slices under grill until golden. Spread half the bread slices with half the sauce; top with artichoke, capsicum, patties, rocket then remaining sauce and remaining bread slices.

ripe tomato sauce Heat oil in medium saucepan; cook garlic, stirring, until fragrant. Add tomato; cook, uncovered, stirring occasionally, about 30 minutes or until sauce thickens slightly. Remove from heat; stir in vinegar.

prep + cook time *40 minutes (+ refrigeration)*
serves *6*
nutritional count per serving *23.8g total fat (8.2g saturated fat); 2412kJ (577 cal); 49.2g carbohydrate; 38.4g protein; 5.3g fibre*

quick chilli con carne

500g beef mince
2 fresh long red chillies, chopped finely
35g packet taco seasoning mix
400g can diced tomatoes
½ cup (125ml) water
420g can kidney beans, rinsed, drained
⅓ cup coarsely chopped fresh coriander

1 Cook mince in heated oiled large frying pan, stirring, until browned. Add chillies and seasoning mix; cook, stirring, until fragrant.
2 Add undrained tomatoes and the water; bring to the boil. Reduce heat; simmer, uncovered, 15 minutes. Add beans; simmer, uncovered, 5 minutes. Remove from heat, stir in coriander. Serve with warm corn tortillas and sour cream, if you like.
prep + cook time **35 minutes**   serves **4**
nutritional count per serving *12.5g total fat (5.2g saturated fat); 1296kJ (310 cal); 16.9g carbohydrate; 24.2g protein; 6.8g fibre*

cottage pie

1 tablespoon olive oil
2 cloves garlic, crushed
1 large brown onion (200g), chopped finely
2 medium carrots (240g), peeled, chopped finely
1kg beef mince
1 tablespoon worcestershire sauce
2 tablespoons tomato paste
2 x 425g cans crushed tomatoes
1 teaspoon dried mixed herbs
200g mushrooms, quartered
1 cup (120g) frozen peas
1kg sebago potatoes, peeled, chopped coarsely
¾ cup (180ml) hot milk
40g butter, softened
½ cup (50g) coarsely grated pizza cheese

1 Heat oil in large saucepan; cook garlic, onion and carrot, stirring, until onion softens. Add beef; cook, stirring, about 10 minutes or until changed in colour.
2 Add sauce, paste, undrained tomatoes and herbs; bring to the boil. Reduce heat; simmer, uncovered, about 30 minutes or until mixture thickens slightly. Stir in mushrooms and peas.
3 Meanwhile, preheat oven to 180°C/160°C fan-forced.
4 Boil, steam or microwave potato until tender; drain. Mash potato in large bowl with milk and butter.
5 Pour beef mixture into deep 3-litre (12-cup) ovenproof dish, top with mashed potato mixture; sprinkle with cheese. Bake, uncovered, about 45 minutes or until pie is heated through and top is browned lightly.

prep + cook time *1 hour 55 minutes* serves *8*
nutritional count per serving *16.5g total fat (7.6g saturated fat); 1659kJ (397 cal); 23.9g carbohydrate; 35.1g protein; 6g fibre*

You can make the cottage pie up to 2 days in advance; keep, covered, in refrigerator. Reheat, covered, in preheated 160°C/140°C fan-forced oven for about 40 minutes. The pie can also be frozen for up to 3 months; thaw overnight in the refrigerator before reheating as above.

pork & veal lasagne

The great thing about lasagne is you can either make both sauces a day ahead, then assemble the lasagne when you're ready, or completely finish the lasagne a day ahead, put it in the refrigerator and reheat it in the oven (180°C/160°C fan-forced), covered, for about 30 minutes. Or, if you like, freeze the finished lasagne, as a whole, or in serving-sized portions. The whole lasagne will take about 24 hours to thaw in the refrigerator. Individual portions can be thawed in a microwave oven – follow the manufacturer's directions. Pizza cheese (375g) is a good substitute for the parmesan and mozzarella in this recipe.

1 tablespoon olive oil
1 medium brown onion (150g), chopped coarsely
3 trimmed celery stalks (300g), chopped coarsely
4 cloves garlic, crushed
2 teaspoons ground cinnamon
800g pork and veal mince
1 tablespoon plain flour
2 tablespoons red wine vinegar
2 teaspoons brown sugar
700ml bottled tomato pasta sauce
400g can diced tomatoes
¼ cup finely chopped fresh sage
40g butter
2 tablespoons plain flour, extra
2½ cups (625ml) hot milk
1½ cups (120g) finely grated parmesan cheese
250g fresh lasagne sheets
2½ cups (250g) coarsely grated mozzarella cheese
12 fresh sage leaves

1 Heat oil in large saucepan; cook onion and celery, stirring, until soft. Add garlic and cinnamon; cook, stirring, until fragrant.
2 Add mince; cook, stirring, until meat changes colour. Add flour; cook, stirring, 1 minute. Stir in vinegar, sugar, pasta sauce and undrained tomatoes; bring to the boil. Reduce heat; simmer, stirring occasionally, about 15 minutes or until sauce thickens. Stir in chopped sage.
3 Preheat oven to 180°C/160°C fan-forced.
4 Meanwhile, melt butter in medium saucepan. Add extra flour; cook, stirring, until mixture thickens and bubbles. Gradually stir in milk; stir until mixture boils and thickens. Remove sauce from heat; stir in one-third of the parmesan.
5 Spread a quarter of the meat sauce into shallow 20cm x 31cm ovenproof dish. Cover with one-third of the trimmed lasagne sheets, then one-third of the remaining meat sauce, half the cheese sauce and half the mozzarella. Make two more layers with the remaining lasagne and meat sauce; top with remaining cheese sauce then sprinkle with combined remaining cheeses. Sprinkle with sage leaves. Cook, uncovered, in oven, about 50 minutes or until browned lightly. Stand lasagne 15 minutes before serving. Serve with a mesclun salad, if you like.

prep + cook time *1 hour 30 minutes (+ standing)*
serves *6*
nutritional count per serving *39.3g total fat (20.5g saturated fat); 3428kJ (820 cal); 55.2g carbohydrate; 58.3g protein; 6.3g fibre*

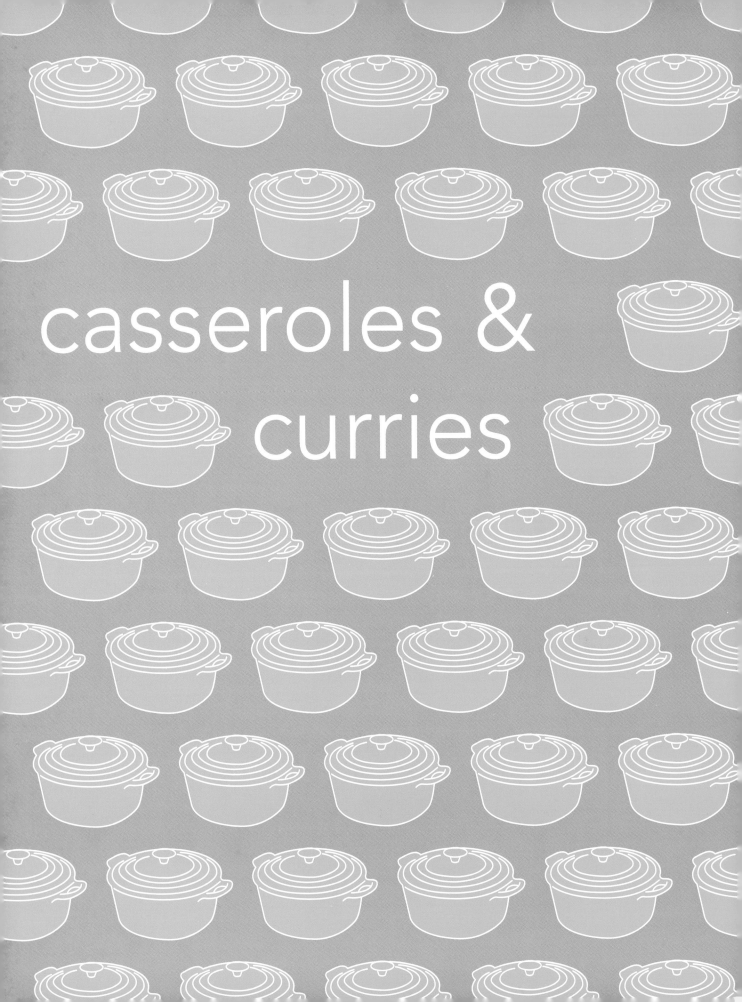

casseroles & curries

beef burgundy

300g baby brown onions
2 tablespoons olive oil
2kg gravy beef, trimmed, chopped coarsely
30g butter
4 rindless bacon rashers (260g), chopped coarsely
400g button mushrooms, halved
2 cloves garlic, crushed
¼ cup (35g) plain flour
1¼ cups (310ml) beef stock
2½ cups (625ml) dry red wine
2 bay leaves
2 sprigs fresh thyme
½ cup coarsely chopped fresh flat-leaf parsley

1 Peel onions, leaving root end intact so onion remains whole during cooking.
2 Heat oil in large flameproof dish; cook beef, in batches, until browned.
3 Add butter to dish; cook onions, bacon, mushrooms and garlic, stirring, until onions are browned lightly.
4 Sprinkle flour over onion mixture; cook, stirring, until flour mixture thickens and bubbles. Gradually add stock and wine; stir over heat until mixture boils and thickens. Return beef and any juices to dish, add bay leaves and thyme; bring to the boil. Reduce heat; simmer, covered, about 2 hours or until beef is tender, stirring every 30 minutes.
5 Remove from heat; discard bay leaves. Stir in parsley.

prep + cook time *2 hours 45 minutes*   **serves** *6*
nutritional count per serving *31.4g total fat (12.1g saturated fat); 2658kJ (636 cal); 6.6g carbohydrate; 80.3g protein; 2.8g fibre*

beef & mushrooms in red wine

2 tablespoons olive oil
1kg beef blade steak, diced into 2cm pieces
4 medium brown onions (600g), chopped coarsely
200g mushrooms, halved
2⅓ cups (580ml) dry red wine
¼ cup (60ml) beef stock
2 x 410g cans crushed tomatoes
1 tablespoon brown sugar
3 sprigs fresh rosemary
2 tablespoons fresh oregano leaves

1 Heat half the oil in large flameproof casserole dish; cook beef, in batches, until browned.
2 Heat remaining oil in same pan; cook onion, stirring, 2 minutes. Add mushrooms; cook, stirring, 2 minutes.
3 Return beef to pan with wine, stock, undrained tomatoes, sugar, rosemary and half the oregano; bring to the boil. Reduce heat; simmer, covered, 1 hour, stirring occasionally. Uncover; simmer 15 minutes. Serve beef sprinkled with remaining oregano, and accompanied with ciabatta bread.
prep + cook time *1 hour 45 minutes*   **serves 4**
nutritional count per serving *26g total fat (8.3g saturated fat); 2332kJ (558 cal); 17.7g carbohydrate; 58.1g protein; 5.7g fibre*

provençale beef
casserole

2 tablespoons olive oil
1kg gravy beef, cut into 2cm pieces
2 rindless bacon rashers (130g), chopped finely
1 medium leek (350g), sliced thinly
2 medium carrots (240g), chopped coarsely
1 trimmed celery stalk (100g), chopped coarsely
2 cloves garlic, crushed
410g can crushed tomatoes
1½ cups (375ml) beef stock
1 cup (250ml) dry red wine
2 bay leaves
4 sprigs fresh thyme
6 sprigs fresh flat-leaf parsley
2 medium zucchini (240g), sliced thickly
½ cup (75g) seeded black olives

1 Heat oil in large saucepan; cook beef, in batches, until browned.
2 Cook bacon, leek, carrot, celery and garlic in same pan, stirring, until leek softens.
3 Return beef to pan with undrained tomatoes, stock, wine, bay leaves, thyme and parsley; bring to the boil. Reduce heat; simmer, covered, 1 hour, stirring occasionally.
4 Add zucchini and olives; simmer, covered, about 30 minutes or until beef is tender.
5 Remove and discard bay leaves, thyme and parsley before serving with crushed kipfler potatoes.

prep + cook time *2 hours 30 minutes* serves *4*
nutritional count per serving *25.8g total fat (7.8g saturated fat); 2458kJ (588 cal); 14.1g carbohydrate; 61.4g protein; 6.4g fibre*

Turn off the oven a few minutes before the recipe states to save on energy. There will be enough heat in the oven to complete the cooking.

beef & wine stew with yorkshire puddings

800g beef chuck steak, cut into 4cm pieces
2 tablespoons plain flour
⅓ cup (80ml) olive oil
40g butter
6 shallots (150g), halved
2 cloves garlic, crushed
150g button mushrooms, halved
1 large carrot (180g), chopped coarsely
1 cup (250ml) dry red wine
2 tablespoons tomato paste
1 cup (250ml) beef stock
2 tablespoons worcestershire sauce
2 sprigs fresh thyme
¼ cup coarsely chopped fresh chives

yorkshire pudding batter
⅓ cup (50g) plain flour
¼ teaspoon salt
⅓ cup (80ml) milk
1 egg

1 Coat beef in flour; shake off excess. Heat 2 tablespoons of the oil in large saucepan; cook beef, in batches, until browned all over.
2 Melt half the butter in same pan; cook shallot, garlic, mushrooms and carrot, stirring, until vegetables soften. Add wine; bring to the boil. Return beef to pan with paste, stock, sauce and thyme; bring to the boil. Reduce heat; simmer, covered, 1¼ hours. Uncover; simmer about 15 minutes or until sauce thickens. Stir in chives.
3 Meanwhile, make yorkshire pudding batter.
4 Preheat oven to 240°C/220°C fan-forced.
5 Melt remaining butter; divide combined melted butter and remaining oil among four holes of six-hole (¾-cup/180ml) texas muffin pan. Heat pan in oven 3 minutes. Remove pan from oven; immediately divide batter among hot pan holes. Return pan to oven; bake about 12 minutes or until puddings are well browned. Serve puddings, top-side up, with stew; sprinkle with chopped fresh chives, if you like.
yorkshire pudding batter Sift flour and salt into small bowl. Whisk in combined milk and egg until smooth. Pour into jug, cover; stand 20 minutes.
prep + cook time *2 hours 15 minutes* serves **4**
nutritional count per serving *38.2g total fat (12.8g saturated fat); 2788kJ (667 cal); 21.1g carbohydrate; 48.4g protein; 4.1g fibre*

Frozen vegetables are best purchased in bags rather than in boxes. The bags allow you to easily re-seal the opening.

rabbit stew

2 tablespoons oil
1kg rabbit pieces
3 medium brown onions (450g), sliced thickly
4 cloves garlic, crushed
1 cup (250ml) water
1 litre (4 cups) chicken stock
410g can diced tomatoes
5 medium potatoes (1kg), chopped coarsely
2 medium carrots (240g), sliced thickly
1 tablespoon balsamic vinegar
3 bay leaves
1 teaspoon dried chilli flakes
⅓ cup coarsely chopped fresh mint
1 cup (120g) frozen peas

1 Heat half the oil in large saucepan; cook rabbit, in batches, until browned.
2 Heat remaining oil in same pan; cook onion and garlic, stirring, until onion softens.
3 Add the water, stock, undrained tomatoes, potato, carrot, vinegar, bay leaves, chilli and mint to pan. Return rabbit to pan; bring to the boil. Reduce heat; simmer, uncovered, 1¼ hours. Add peas; simmer, uncovered, 5 minutes.
prep + cook time *2 hours 5 minutes* **serves 4**
nutritional count per serving *19.4g total fat (5.1g saturated fat); 2750kJ (658 cal); 44.4g carbohydrate; 70.7g protein; 10.6g fibre*

This stew is not suitable to freeze.

pork neck, orange & white bean stew

1 tablespoon olive oil

800g pork neck, cut into 3cm pieces

1 large celeriac (750g), trimmed, peeled, chopped coarsely

3 medium carrots (360g), chopped coarsely

3 cloves garlic, peeled

1 cup (250ml) dry white wine

1 cup (250ml) chicken stock

3 x 5cm strips orange rind

½ cup (125ml) orange juice

400g can cannellini beans, rinsed, drained

1 Heat oil in large flameproof casserole dish; cook pork, in batches, until browned. Add vegetables, garlic, wine, stock, rind and juice to dish; bring to the boil. Return pork to dish, reduce heat; simmer, covered, 40 minutes.

2 Add beans to dish; simmer, uncovered, about 20 minutes or until pork is tender.

prep + cook time *1 hour 40 minutes* serves 4
nutritional count per serving *21.4g total fat (6.2g saturated fat); 2215kJ (530 cal); 18.1g carbohydrate; 50g protein; 12.7g fibre*

This stew is not suitable to freeze.

Contrary to other food items, buy fresh spices in the smallest quantities possible because they lose their flavour quickly.

chilli con carne

1 cup (200g) dried kidney beans

1.5kg beef chuck steak

2 litres (8 cups) water

1 tablespoon olive oil

2 medium brown onions (300g), chopped coarsely

2 cloves garlic, crushed

2 teaspoons ground cumin

2 teaspoons ground coriander

½ teaspoon cayenne pepper

2 teaspoons sweet paprika

2 x 400g cans crushed tomatoes

1 tablespoon tomato paste

4 green onions, chopped coarsely

2 tablespoons coarsely chopped fresh coriander

⅓ cup (65g) finely chopped bottled jalapeño chillies

1 Place beans in medium bowl, cover with water; stand overnight, drain.

2 Combine beef with the water in large saucepan; bring to the boil. Reduce heat, simmer, covered, 1½ hours.

3 Drain beef in large muslin-lined strainer over bowl; reserve 3½ cups (875ml) of the cooking liquid. Using two forks, shred beef.

4 Heat oil in same pan; cook brown onion and garlic, stirring, until onion is soft. Add spices; cook, stirring, until fragrant. Add beans, undrained tomatoes, paste and 2 cups of the reserved liquid; bring to the boil. Reduce heat, simmer, covered, 1 hour.

5 Add beef and remaining reserved liquid to pan; simmer, covered, about 30 minutes or until beans are tender. Remove from heat; stir in green onions, coriander and chilli. Serve chilli con carne with steamed rice, if you like.

prep + cook time *3 hours 45 minutes (+ standing)*
serves *8*
nutritional count per serving *11.4g total fat (3.9g saturated fat); 1496kJ (358 cal); 14.7g carbohydrate; 45.1g protein; 7.6g fibre*

country-style beef & potato casserole

This casserole is not suitable to freeze.

1kg beef chuck steak, cut into 2cm pieces
½ cup (75g) plain flour, approximately
2 tablespoons olive oil
3 small brown onions (450g), halved
2 cloves garlic, crushed
2 rindless bacon rashers (130g), chopped coarsely
2 tablespoons tomato paste
3 cups (750ml) beef stock
410g can crushed tomatoes
¼ cup (60ml) worcestershire sauce
2 medium potatoes (400g), chopped coarsely
1 medium kumara (400g), chopped coarsely
1 large red capsicum (350g), chopped coarsely
1 tablespoon coarsely chopped fresh thyme

1 Coat beef in flour, shake away excess. Heat oil in large saucepan; cook beef, in batches, until browned.
2 Cook onion, garlic and bacon in same pan, stirring, until bacon crisps. Add paste; cook, stirring, 1 minute.
3 Return beef to pan with stock, undrained tomatoes and sauce; bring to the boil. Reduce heat; simmer, covered, 1 hour, stirring occasionally.
4 Add potato, kumara and capsicum to pan; simmer, uncovered, stirring occasionally, about 30 minutes or until beef is tender. Serve sprinkled with thyme.
prep + cook time *2 hours 35 minutes*   serves *6*
nutritional count per serving   *17.3g total fat (5.2g saturated fat); 2036kJ (487 cal); 34.5g carbohydrate; 45.5g protein; 4.8g fibre*

harissa & mint
vegetable stew

40g butter
10 shallots (250g), halved
6 cloves garlic, crushed
2 tablespoons plain flour
2 cups (500ml) vegetable stock
2 cups (500ml) water
1kg new potatoes, halved
410g can crushed tomatoes
2 tablespoons harissa paste
1 cinnamon stick
½ cup firmly packed fresh mint leaves
500g yellow patty-pan squash, halved
115g baby corn
½ cup (60g) frozen peas
250g cherry tomatoes, halved

1 Heat butter in large saucepan; cook shallot and garlic, stirring, until shallot softens. Add flour; cook, stirring, 1 minute.
2 Add stock, the water, potato, undrained tomatoes, harissa, cinnamon and about two-thirds of the mint leaves to pan; bring to the boil. Reduce heat; simmer, uncovered, 30 minutes.
3 Add squash to pan; simmer, uncovered, 20 minutes. Add corn, peas and cherry tomato; simmer, uncovered, 10 minutes. Serve stew sprinkled with remaining mint.

prep + cook time *1 hour 30 minutes*   serves *4*
nutritional count per serving   *10.3g total fat (5.7g saturated fat); 1705kJ (408 cal); 55.7g carbohydrate; 15.7g protein; 14.3g fibre*

This stew is not suitable to freeze.

Use fresh tomatoes when they are plentiful and inexpensive, instead of canned. To prepare them for cooking, cut a cross in the base of each tomato and place in a heatproof bowl. Pour boiling water over them and leave for a few minutes. Peel back the skin, then add them whole, chopped or crushed, to a casserole or soup.

beef & bean casserole

2 tablespoons olive oil

1kg beef chuck steak, cut into 2cm pieces

2 medium brown onions (300g), chopped finely

2 cloves garlic, crushed

1 teaspoon ground turmeric

2 teaspoons ground cumin

½ teaspoon dried chilli flakes

¼ cup (70g) tomato paste

410g can crushed tomatoes

2 cups (500ml) beef stock

2 bay leaves

2 medium potatoes (400g), chopped coarsely

400g can kidney beans, rinsed, drained

¼ cup coarsely chopped fresh coriander

¼ cup coarsely chopped fresh flat-leaf parsley

1 Heat oil in large saucepan; cook beef, in batches, until browned.

2 Add onion and garlic to pan; cook, stirring, until onion softens. Add spices; cook, stirring, until fragrant. Add paste; cook, stirring, 1 minute.

3 Return beef to pan with undrained tomatoes, stock and bay leaves; bring to the boil. Reduce heat; simmer, covered, 1 hour.

4 Add potato to pan; simmer, uncovered, about 30 minutes or until potato is tender.

5 Discard bay leaves. Add beans to pan; stir until heated through. Remove from heat, stir through herbs.

prep + cook time *2 hours 20 minutes* **serves** *4*
nutritional count per serving *21.4g total fat (6.2g saturated fat); 2383kJ (570 cal); 28.8g carbohydrate; 60.8g protein; 8.9g fibre*

Make your own stock. Fresh stock is not only cheaper but it will be fresh and have more flavour than stock cubes. Stock can be frozen for up to six months. Freeze in ice-cube containers then transfer to strong plastic bags – use as required.

irish stew

750g lamb neck chops
2 large brown onions (400g), chopped coarsely
1 large carrot (180g), chopped coarsely
1 large parsnip (350g), chopped coarsely
1kg potatoes, chopped coarsely
3½ cups (625ml) beef stock
2 tablespoons tomato paste
1 tablespoon worcestershire sauce
2 sprigs thyme
¼ cup coarsely chopped fresh flat-leaf parsley

1 Preheat oven to 160°C/140°C fan-forced.
2 Layer chops and vegetables in large ovenproof dish; pour over combined stock, paste and sauce. Add thyme.
3 Cook, covered, 2 hours. Uncover; cook 30 minutes or until lamb and vegetables are tender. Serve stew sprinkled with parsley.
prep + cook time *3 hours*   serves *4*
nutritional count per serving   *19.3g total fat (8.6g saturated fat); 2249kJ (538 cal); 46.8g carbohydrate; 39.7g protein; 8.5g fibre*

Choose fresh vegetables over canned or frozen –
they are usually cheaper and more nutritious.

curried sausages

800g thick beef sausages
20g butter
1 medium brown onion (150g), chopped coarsely
1 tablespoon curry powder
2 teaspoons plain flour
2 large carrots (360g), chopped coarsely
2 trimmed celery stalks (200g), chopped coarsely
500g new potatoes, halved
2 cups (500ml) beef stock
1 cup loosely packed fresh flat-leaf parsley leaves

1 Cook sausages, in batches, in heated deep large
frying pan until cooked through. Cut each sausage
into thirds.
2 Melt butter in same cleaned pan; cook onion,
stirring, until soft. Add curry powder and flour;
cook, stirring, 2 minutes.
3 Add vegetables and stock; bring to the boil.
Reduce heat; simmer, covered, about 15 minutes or
until vegetables are tender. Add sausages; simmer,
uncovered, until sauce thickens slightly. Stir in parsley.
prep + cook time *55 minutes*   **serves** *4*
nutritional count per serving *55.8g total fat
(27.3g saturated fat); 3177kJ (760 cal); 29.8g
carbohydrate; 30.1g protein; 12.8g fibre*

Grow your own herbs in kitchen window boxes. Rosemary, basil, parsley and thyme are popular and can be used in many dishes. Pick fresh herbs when required.

braised lamb shanks
with white bean puree

1 tablespoon olive oil
8 french-trimmed lamb shanks (2kg)
1 large red onion (300g), chopped coarsely
2 cloves garlic, crushed
1 cup (250ml) chicken stock
2 cups (500ml) water
400g can diced tomatoes
1 tablespoon fresh rosemary leaves
4 drained anchovy fillets, chopped coarsely
2 large red capsicums (700g)
2 large green capsicums (700g)

white bean puree
20g butter
1 small brown onion (80g), chopped finely
1 clove garlic, crushed
¼ cup (60ml) dry white wine
¾ cup (180ml) chicken stock
2 x 400g cans white beans, rinsed, drained
2 tablespoons cream

1 Heat oil in large deep saucepan; cook lamb, in batches, until browned all over.
2 Cook onion and garlic in same pan, stirring, until onion softens. Add stock, the water, undrained tomatoes, rosemary and anchovy; bring to the boil. Return lamb to pan, reduce heat; simmer, covered, 1 hour, stirring occasionally. Uncover; simmer about 45 minutes or until lamb is tender.
3 Meanwhile, quarter capsicums; discard seeds and membranes. Roast under hot grill or in very hot oven, skin-side up, until skin blisters and blackens. Cover capsicum pieces with plastic wrap or paper for 5 minutes; peel away skin, slice thickly.
4 Meanwhile, make white bean puree.
5 Add capsicum to lamb; cook, uncovered, 5 minutes. Serve lamb on white bean puree.

white bean puree Melt butter in medium frying pan; cook onion and garlic, stirring, until onion softens. Add wine; cook, stirring, until liquid is reduced by half. Add stock and beans; bring to the boil. Reduce heat; simmer, uncovered, about 10 minutes or until liquid is almost evaporated. Blend or process bean mixture and cream until smooth.

prep + cook time *3 hours 10 minutes* serves *4* nutritional count per serving *18.8g* total fat *(8.4g saturated fat); 2312kJ (553 cal); 21g carbohydrate; 72.1g protein; 8.6g fibre*

indian dry beef curry

2 tablespoons peanut oil
2 medium brown onions (300g), chopped coarsely
4 cloves garlic, crushed
4cm piece fresh ginger (20g), grated
2 teaspoons ground cumin
2 teaspoons ground coriander
2 teaspoons ground garam masala
1 teaspoon ground turmeric
1.5kg beef chuck steak, cut into 2cm pieces
1 cup (250ml) beef stock
½ cup (140g) yogurt
¼ cup loosely packed fresh coriander leaves

1 Heat oil in large saucepan; cook onion, garlic, ginger and spices, stirring occasionally, until onion softens. Add beef; cook, stirring, until beef is covered in spice mixture.
2 Add stock to pan; bring to the boil. Reduce heat; simmer, covered, 1 hour, stirring occasionally.
3 Uncover; cook about 30 minutes or until liquid has almost evaporated and beef is tender, stirring occasionally.
4 Serve curry topped with yogurt and sprinkled coriander. Accompany with mango chutney and warm naan or steamed white rice.
prep + cook time *1 hour 55 minutes* **serves** *6*
nutritional count per serving *18.3g total fat (6.4g saturated fat); 1659kJ (397 cal); 4.5g carbohydrate; 53g protein; 1.1g fibre*

A piece of fresh root ginger will keep in the freezer if you wrap it up tightly in foil. When required, unravel the foil, slice off a few pieces, then re-seal the foil.

beef vindaloo curry

2 teaspoons cumin seeds

2 teaspoons garam masala

4 cardamom pods, bruised

1 tablespoon grated fresh ginger

6 cloves garlic, crushed

8 fresh red thai chillies, chopped finely

2 tablespoons white vinegar

1 tablespoon tamarind concentrate

1.5kg chuck steak, cut into 3cm cubes

2 tablespoons ghee

2 large brown onions (400g), chopped finely

1 cinnamon stick

6 cloves

2 teaspoons plain flour

3 cups (750ml) beef stock

1 Place cumin, garam masala and cardamom in large heated dry frying pan; stir over heat until fragrant. Combine roasted spices with ginger, garlic, chilli, vinegar and tamarind in large bowl; add steak, toss to coat steak in marinade. Cover; refrigerate for 1 hour or overnight.

2 Melt ghee in same pan; cook onion, cinnamon and cloves, stirring, until onion is browned lightly. Add steak mixture; cook, stirring, until steak is browned all over. Stir in flour; cook, stirring, 2 minutes. Gradually add stock; bring to the boil, stirring. Reduce heat; simmer, uncovered, 1 hour. Serve vindaloo with dhal, raita and, if desired, a bowl of crisp pappadums, if you like.

prep + cook time *4 hours (+ refrigeration)* **serves** *4*
nutritional count per serving *26.2g total fat (13.1g saturated fat); 2500kJ (598 cal); 8.9g carbohydrate; 8.1g protein; 2.5g fibre*

This curry is best made a day ahead to allow its flavours to develop fully. You could also use round steak or skirt steak in this recipe.

Make a comprehensive shopping list of everything you need for the week, taking note of what you require in the way of staples for the store cupboard.

lamb & lentil stew with kumara & carrot mash

1 cup (200g) brown lentils
1 tablespoon vegetable oil
1.5kg lamb neck chops
2 medium brown onions (300g), chopped coarsely
2 cloves garlic, crushed
4 rindless bacon rashers (260g), chopped coarsely
1 teaspoon caraway seeds
2 teaspoons ground cumin
½ cup (125ml) dry red wine
⅓ cup (90g) tomato paste
2 cups (500ml) beef stock
425g can diced tomatoes
½ cup coarsely chopped fresh coriander

kumara & carrot mash
2 medium kumara (800g), chopped coarsely
2 medium carrots (240g), chopped coarsely
1 teaspoon ground cumin
⅓ cup (80ml) buttermilk

1 Cook lentils in large saucepan of boiling water, uncovered, about 15 minutes or until tender; drain.
2 Preheat oven to 180°C/160°C fan-forced.
3 Meanwhile, heat oil in large flameproof casserole dish; cook chops, in batches, until browned. Cook onion, garlic and bacon in same heated pan, stirring, until onion is just browned and bacon is crisp. Add spices; cook, stirring, until fragrant. Add wine, paste, stock and undrained tomatoes; bring to the boil.
4 Return chops to dish; stir in lentils, Cook, covered, in moderate oven 1 hour 10 minutes.
5 Meanwhile, make kumara and carrot mash.
6 Stir coriander into stew just before serving with kumara and carrot mash.
kumara & carrot mash Boil, steam or microwave kumara and carrot, separately, until tender; drain. Dry-fry cumin in small frying pan until fragrant. Mash vegetables in large bowl with cumin and buttermilk until smooth.
prep + cook time *2 hours 5 minutes* serves *4*
nutritional count per serving *47.9g total fat (19.6g saturated fat); 3896kJ (932 cal); 44.2g carbohydrate; 76.1g protein; 9.9g fibre*

When buying fresh green beans, cauliflower and broccoli in bulk, use what you need on the day then freeze the remainder in small freezer bags for individual servings.

red curry lentils

Serve these lentils with steamed rice and fresh coriander leaves, if you like. Chicken stock can be used in place of the vegetable stock in this recipe.

1 tablespoon olive oil
1 medium brown onion (150g), quartered
2 tablespoons red curry paste
2 x 400g cans brown lentils, rinsed, drained
1 cup (250ml) vegetable stock
200g green beans, halved
2 tablespoons lime juice
⅔ cup (190g) yogurt

1 Heat oil in medium saucepan; cook onion, stirring, until soft. Add paste; cook, stirring, until fragrant. Add lentils and stock; bring to the boil. Reduce heat; simmer, uncovered, about 10 minutes or until stock has thickened. Add beans, simmer 2 minutes. Remove from heat; stir in juice.
2 Divide curry among serving bowls; serve topped with yogurt.
prep + cook time *20 minutes*   **serves** *4*
nutritional count per serving *10.5g total fat (2.2g saturated fat); 865kJ (207 cal); 14.3g carbohydrate; 11g protein; 6g fibre*

harira *(north african lamb stew)*

This recipe is not suitable to freeze.

½ cup (100g) french green lentils
500g diced lamb, cut into 1cm pieces
1 medium brown onion (150g), chopped finely
2 cloves garlic, crushed
½ teaspoon ground cinnamon
½ teaspoon ground ginger
½ teaspoon hot paprika
1 teaspoon ground turmeric
pinch saffron threads
1.5 litres (6 cups) water
400g can chickpeas, rinsed, drained
½ cup (100g) cooked white long-grain rice
3 small egg tomatoes (180g), chopped finely
¼ cup finely chopped fresh flat-leaf parsley

1 Cook lentils, lamb, onion, garlic and spices in large flameproof casserole dish, stirring, until lamb is browned. Add the water; bring to the boil. Reduce heat; simmer, covered, 1 hour.
2 Add chickpeas, rice and tomato to dish; simmer, uncovered, about 20 minutes or until rice is just tender. Stir in parsley.
prep + cook time *1 hour 40 minutes* serves *4*
nutritional count per serving *13.1g total fat (5.3g saturated fat); 1919kJ (459 cal); 41.4g carbohydrate; 39.1g protein; 8.3g fibre*

Save pan juices and sauces to add to stews and casseroles. Store in the refrigerator in an airtight container with a secure lid.

beef stew with parsley dumplings

1kg beef chuck steak, cut into 5cm pieces
2 tablespoons plain flour
2 tablespoons olive oil
20g butter
2 medium brown onions (300g), chopped coarsely
2 cloves garlic, crushed
2 medium carrots (240g), chopped coarsely
1 cup (250ml) dry red wine
2 tablespoons tomato paste
2 cups (500ml) beef stock
4 sprigs fresh thyme

parsley dumplings
1 cup (150g) self-raising flour
50g butter
1 egg, beaten lightly
¼ cup (20g) coarsely grated parmesan cheese
¼ cup finely chopped fresh flat-leaf parsley
⅓ cup (50g) drained sun-dried tomatoes, chopped
¼ cup (60ml) milk

1 Preheat oven to 180°C/160°C fan-forced.
2 Coat beef in flour; shake off excess. Heat oil in large flameproof dish; cook beef, in batches, until browned.
3 Melt butter in same dish; cook onion, garlic and carrot, stirring, until vegetables soften. Add wine; cook, stirring, until liquid reduces to ¼ cup. Return beef with paste, stock and thyme; bring to the boil. Cover; cook in oven 1¾ hours.
4 Meanwhile, make parsley dumpling mixture.
5 Remove dish from oven. Drop level tablespoons of dumpling mixture, about 2cm apart, onto top of stew. Cook, uncovered, about 20 minutes or until dumplings are browned lightly and cooked through.
parsley dumplings Place flour in medium bowl; rub in butter. Stir in egg, cheese, parsley, tomato and enough milk to make a soft, sticky dough.
prep + cook time *2 hours 30 minutes* **serves** *4*
nutritional count per serving *39.7g total fat (17.4g saturated fat); 3457kJ (827 cal); 43g carbohydrate; 63.9g protein; 6.7g fibre*

lentil & vegetable curry

1 tablespoon olive oil
2 medium brown onions (300g), chopped coarsely
1¼ cups (250g) brown lentils
1.25 litres (5 cups) vegetable stock
2 small kumara (500g), cut into 2cm pieces
400g broccoli, cut into florets
2 red banana chillies (250g), chopped coarsely

curry paste
2 long green chillies, chopped coarsely
5 cloves garlic, chopped coarsely
8cm piece fresh ginger (40g), chopped coarsely
1 cup firmly packed fresh coriander leaves
1 tablespoon olive oil

1 Make curry paste.
2 Heat oil in large saucepan; cook onion, stirring, until softened. Stir in curry paste; cook, stirring, until fragrant.
3 Add lentils and stock to pan; bring to the boil. Reduce heat; simmer, uncovered, 10 minutes. Stir in kumara; simmer, covered, 10 minutes. Stir in broccoli and chilli; simmer, covered, about 5 minutes or until lentils and vegetables are tender.
curry paste Blend or process ingredients until almost smooth.
prep + cook time *45 minutes* **serves 6**
nutritional count per serving *8.3g total fat (1.4g saturated fat); 1283kJ (307 cal); 32.9g carbohydrate; 18.7g protein; 12.4g fibre*

This curry is at its best eaten just after making it – the vegetables will discolour and become mushy if the curry is made in advance. To save time, make the curry paste and chop the vegetables up to a day ahead. Serve with steamed basmati rice and combined yogurt and coarsely chopped fresh coriander, if you like.

slow-roasted honey & soy pork neck

1 tablespoon peanut oil
1kg piece pork neck
1 large brown onion (200g), sliced thinly
2 cloves garlic, sliced thinly
4cm piece fresh ginger (20g), sliced thinly
1 cinnamon stick
2 star anise
½ cup (125ml) salt-reduced soy sauce
½ cup (125ml) chinese cooking wine
¼ cup (90g) honey
1 cup (250ml) water
450g baby buk choy, trimmed, leaves separated

1 Preheat oven to 160°C/140°C fan-forced.
2 Heat oil in large flameproof casserole dish; cook pork, turning occasionally, until browned. Remove from dish. Add onion, garlic and ginger to same dish; cook, uncovered, until onion softens. Remove from heat.
3 Stir cinnamon, star anise, sauce, cooking wine, honey and the water into onion mixture in dish. Return pork to dish, turning to coat in spice mixture. Cover dish; transfer to oven. Cook 1 hour. Uncover; cook about 1 hour or until sauce thickens slightly. Remove pork from dish. Cover pork; stand 10 minutes before slicing.
4 Add buk choy to dish; cook, over heat, stirring, about 5 minutes or until just tender. Serve pork with buk choy and sauce.

prep + cook time **1 hour 35 minutes** serves **4**
nutritional count per serving **30.6g total fat (9.8g saturated fat); 2621kJ (627 cal); 5.9g carbohydrate; 76.4g protein; 2.5g fibre**

Use the cheapest cuts of meat for casseroles or braised dishes. Make your own rubs and marinades – it's much cheaper than bought ones.

massaman curry

1kg skirt steak, cut into 3cm pieces
2 cups (500ml) beef stock
5 cardamom pods, bruised
¼ teaspoon ground clove
2 star anise
1 tablespoon grated palm sugar
2 tablespoons fish sauce
2 tablespoons tamarind concentrate
2 x 400ml cans coconut milk
2 tablespoons massaman curry paste
8 baby brown onions (200g), halved
1 medium kumara (400g), chopped coarsely
¼ cup (35g) coarsely chopped roasted
    unsalted peanuts
2 green onions, sliced thinly

1 Place beef, 1½ cups of the stock, cardamom, clove, star anise, sugar, sauce, 1 tablespoon of the tamarind and half of the coconut milk in large saucepan; simmer, uncovered, about 1½ hours or until beef is almost tender.
2 Strain beef over large bowl; reserve braising liquid, discard solids. Cover beef to keep warm.
3 Cook curry paste in same pan, stirring, until fragrant. Add remaining coconut milk, tamarind and stock; bring to the boil. Cook, stirring, about 1 minute or until mixture is smooth. Return beef to pan with brown onion, kumara and 1 cup of the reserved braising liquid; simmer, uncovered, about 30 minutes or until beef and vegetables are tender.
4 Stir nuts and green onion into curry off the heat.
prep + cook time *2 hours 30 minutes*   serves *4*
nutritional count per serving *52.7g total fat (39.5g saturated fat); 3645kJ (872 cal); 29.2g carbohydrate; 67.4g protein; 7.2g fibre*

red chicken curry
with snow peas

Red curry paste is available in various strengths in many supermarkets; adjust the amount to suit your palate.

1 tablespoon vegetable oil
800g chicken thigh fillets, chopped coarsely
2 tablespoons red curry paste
400ml can coconut cream
150g sugar snap peas, trimmed
⅓ cup firmly packed fresh coriander leaves

1 Heat half the oil in large saucepan; cook chicken, in batches, until browned.
2 Heat remaining oil in same pan; cook paste, stirring, about 3 minutes or until fragrant.
3 Return chicken to pan with coconut cream; bring to the boil. Reduce heat; simmer, uncovered, 10 minutes or until chicken is cooked through.
4 Add peas to pan; simmer, uncovered, 1 minute or until tender.
5 Serve curry sprinkled with coriander. Accompany with steamed jasmine rice, if you like.

prep + cook time *30 minutes*   serves *4*
nutritional count per serving *43.4g total fat (23.5g saturated fat); 2433kJ (582 cal); 6.5g carbohydrate; 41g protein; 3g fibre*

beef rendang

1.5kg beef chuck steak, trimmed,
   cut into 3cm cubes
400ml can coconut milk
½ cup (125ml) water
10cm stick fresh lemon grass (20g), bruised
3 fresh kaffir lime leaves, torn

spice paste
2 medium red onions (340g), chopped coarsely
4 cloves garlic, chopped coarsely
5cm piece fresh ginger (25g), chopped coarsely
2 fresh long red chillies, chopped coarsely
3 teaspoons grated fresh galangal
3 teaspoons ground coriander
1½ teaspoons ground cumin
1 teaspoon ground turmeric
1 teaspoon salt

1 Blend or process spice paste ingredients until combined.
2 Combine paste in wok with beef, coconut milk, the water, lemon grass and lime leaves; bring to the boil. Reduce heat; simmer, covered, stirring occasionally, about 2 hours or until mixture thickens and beef is tender.
prep + cook time *2 hours 15 minutes*   **serves** *6*
nutritional count per serving *25.2g total fat (16.9g saturated fat); 1952kJ (467 cal); 6.1g carbohydrate; 52.9g protein; 2.5g fibre*

Serve with steamed jasmine rice, accompanied by combined finely chopped cucumber and finely sliced fresh red chilli in rice vinegar. You can make the curry a day or two before you need it.

Meat is usually the most expensive item on an everyday shopping list but it is the easiest place to save money. Buy your favourite cuts in bulk and freeze in handy portion sizes.

rogan josh

2 teaspoons ground cardamom

2 teaspoons ground cumin

2 teaspoons ground coriander

1kg boned leg of lamb, trimmed, cut into 3cm pieces

20g butter

2 tablespoons vegetable oil

2 medium brown onions (300g), sliced thinly

4cm piece fresh ginger (20g), grated

4 cloves garlic, crushed

2 teaspoons sweet paprika

½ teaspoon cayenne pepper

½ cup (125ml) beef stock

425g can crushed tomatoes

2 bay leaves

2 cinnamon sticks

200g yogurt

¾ cup (110g) roasted slivered almonds

1 fresh long red chilli, sliced thinly

cucumber raita

1 cup (280g) thick "country-style" yogurt

1 lebanese cucumber (130g), seeded, chopped finely

1 tablespoon finely chopped fresh mint

pinch ground cumin

1 Combine cardamom, cumin and coriander in medium bowl, add lamb; toss lamb to coat in spice mixture.

2 Heat butter and half of the oil in large deep saucepan; cook lamb, in batches, until browned all over.

3 Heat remaining oil in same pan; cook onion, ginger, garlic, paprika and cayenne over low heat, stirring, until onion softens.

4 Return lamb to pan with stock, undrained tomatoes, bay leaves and cinnamon. Add yogurt, 1 tablespoon at a time, stirring well between each addition; bring to the boil. Reduce heat; simmer, covered, about 1½ hours or until lamb is tender.

5 Meanwhile, make cucumber raita.

6 Sprinkle lamb with nuts and chilli off the heat; serve with raita and, if you like, warmed naan bread.

cucumber raita Combine yogurt, cucumber and mint in small bowl with salt, pepper and cumin to taste.

prep + cook time *2 hours 20 minutes* serves *4*
nutritional count per serving (incl. raita)
48.1g total fat (15.3g saturated fat); 3219kJ (770 cal); 15.7g carbohydrate; 68.9g protein; 5.5g fibre

sweet things

college pudding

⅓ cup (110g) raspberry jam
1 egg
½ cup (110g) caster sugar
1 cup (150g) self-raising flour
½ cup (125ml) milk
25g butter, melted
1 tablespoon boiling water
1 teaspoon vanilla extract

1 Grease four 1-cup (250ml) metal moulds; divide jam among moulds.
2 Beat egg and sugar in small bowl with electric mixer until thick and creamy. Fold in sifted flour and milk, in two batches; fold in combined butter, the water and extract.
3 Top jam with pudding mixture. Cover each mould with pleated baking paper and foil (to allow puddings to expand as they cook); secure with kitchen string.
4 Place puddings in large saucepan with enough boiling water to come halfway up sides of moulds. Cover pan with tight-fitting lid; boil 25 minutes, replenishing water as necessary to maintain level. Stand puddings 5 minutes before turning onto plate. Serve with cream, if you like.

prep + cook time *40 minutes*   serves **4**
nutritional count per serving *8.1g total fat (4.7g saturated fat); 1676kJ (401 cal); 73.7g carbohydrate; 6.5g protein; 1.7g fibre*

golden syrup
dumplings

1¼ cups (185g) self-raising flour
30g butter
⅓ cup (115g) golden syrup
⅓ cup (80ml) milk

sauce
30g butter
¾ cup (165g) firmly packed brown sugar
½ cup (175g) golden syrup
1⅔ cups (410ml) water

1 Sift flour into medium bowl; rub in butter. Gradually stir in golden syrup and milk.
2 Make sauce.
3 Drop rounded tablespoonfuls of mixture into simmering sauce; simmer, covered, about 20 minutes. Serve dumplings with sauce.
sauce Stir ingredients in medium saucepan over heat, without boiling, until sugar dissolves. Bring to the boil, without stirring. Reduce heat; simmer, uncovered, 5 minutes.

prep + cook time **35 minutes**   serves **4**
nutritional count per serving **13.6g total fat (8.7g saturated fat); 2788kJ (667cal); 128.3g carbohydrate; 5.6g protein; 1.8g fibre**

ginger sticky date pudding

1 cup (140g) seeded dried dates
¼ cup (55g) glacé ginger
1 teaspoon bicarbonate of soda
1 cup (250ml) boiling water
50g butter, chopped
½ cup (110g) firmly packed brown sugar
2 eggs
1 cup (150g) self-raising flour
1 teaspoon ground ginger

butterscotch sauce
300ml cream
¾ cup (165g) firmly packed brown sugar
75g butter, chopped

1 Preheat oven to 200°C/180°C fan-forced. Grease deep 20cm-round cake pan; line base with baking paper.
2 Combine dates, ginger, soda and the water in food processor; stand 5 minutes then add butter and sugar. Process until mixture is almost smooth. Add eggs, flour and ginger; process until combined.
3 Pour mixture into pan; bake about 45 minutes. Stand 10 minutes before turning onto serving plate.
4 Meanwhile, make butterscotch sauce. Serve pudding warm with sauce.
butterscotch sauce Stir ingredients in medium saucepan over low heat until sauce is smooth.
prep + cook time **55 minutes** serves **8**
nutritional count per serving **30.1g total fat (19.6g saturated fat); 2337kJ (559 cal); 65.1g carbohydrate; 4.7g protein; 2.4g fibre**

creamed rice

1 litre (4 cups) milk
⅓ cup (75g) caster sugar
1 teaspoon vanilla extract
½ cup (100g) uncooked white medium-grain rice

1 Combine milk, sugar and extract in large saucepan; bring to the boil. Gradually add rice to boiling milk. Reduce heat; simmer, covered, stirring occasionally, about 50 minutes or until rice is tender and milk is almost absorbed.
2 Serve warm or cold, with fresh berries, if desired.
prep + cook time *55 minutes* **serves 4**
nutritional count per serving *9.9g total fat (6.4g saturated fat); 1400kJ (335 cal); 50.6g carbohydrate; 16.1g protein; 0.2g fibre*

bread & butter pudding

6 slices white bread (270g)
40g butter, softened
½ cup (80g) sultanas
¼ teaspoon ground nutmeg

custard
1½ cups (375ml) milk
2 cups (500ml) cream
⅓ cup (75g) caster sugar
1 teaspoon vanilla extract
4 eggs

1 Preheat oven to 160°C/140°C fan-forced. Grease shallow 2-litre (8-cup) ovenproof dish.
2 Make custard.
3 Trim crusts from bread. Spread each slice with butter; cut into four triangles. Layer bread, overlapping, in dish; sprinkle with sultanas. Pour custard over bread; sprinkle with nutmeg.
4 Place ovenproof dish in large baking dish; add enough boiling water to come halfway up side of ovenproof dish. Bake about 45 minutes or until pudding is set. Remove pudding from baking dish; stand 5 minutes before serving.
custard Combine milk, cream, sugar and extract in medium saucepan; bring to the boil. Whisk eggs in large bowl; whisking constantly, gradually add hot milk mixture to egg mixture.

prep + cook time *1 hour 15 minutes* **serves** *6*
nutritional count per serving *48.6g total fat (30.4g saturated fat); 2859kJ (684 cal); 49.3g carbohydrate; 12.4g protein; 1.8g fibre*

You can serve this pudding dusted with sifted icing sugar, if you like.

Do not throw away over-ripe bananas. Slice a banana, squeeze lemon juice over the slices, place in a small plastic bag. Freeze for later use in milkshakes and desserts.

banoffee pie

395g can sweetened condensed milk
75g butter, chopped
½ cup (110g) firmly packed brown sugar
2 tablespoons golden syrup
2 large bananas (460g), sliced thinly
300ml thickened cream, whipped

pastry
1½ cups (225g) plain flour
1 tablespoon icing sugar
140g cold butter, chopped
1 egg yolk
2 tablespoons cold water

1 Make pastry.
2 Grease 24cm-round loose-based fluted flan tin. Roll dough between sheets of baking paper until large enough to line tin. Ease dough into tin; press into base and side. Trim edge; prick base all over with fork. Cover; refrigerate 30 minutes.
3 Preheat oven to 200°C/180°C fan-forced.
4 Place tin on oven tray; cover dough with baking paper, fill with dried beans or rice. Bake 10 minutes; remove paper and beans carefully from pie shell. Bake a further 10 minutes; cool.
5 Meanwhile, combine condensed milk, butter, sugar and syrup in medium saucepan; cook over medium heat, stirring, about 10 minutes or until mixture is caramel-coloured. Stand 5 minutes; pour into pie shell, cool.
6 Top caramel with banana; top with whipped cream.
pastry Process flour, sugar and butter until crumbly; add egg yolk and water, process until ingredients come together. Knead dough on floured surface until smooth. Wrap in plastic; refrigerate 30 minutes.
prep + cook time *1 hour 20 minutes (+ refrigeration)*
serves *8*
nutritional information per serving *41.6g total fat (27g saturated fat); 3005kJ (719 cal); 76.3g carbohydrate; 9.2g protein; 1.9g fibre*

caramelised bananas

100g butter
⅓ cup (75g) firmly packed brown sugar
¾ cup (165g) caster sugar
2 tablespoons water
½ cup (125ml) cream
4 large ripe bananas (920g), sliced thickly

1 Heat butter in large frying pan; add sugars and the water. Stir over heat, without boiling, until sugar dissolves; stir in cream. Bring to the boil; add banana, stir gently to coat in caramel.
2 Serve with cream or ice-cream, if you like.
prep + cook time *15 minutes*   serves *4*
nutritional count per serving *34.2g total fat (22.4g saturated fat); 2893kJ (692 cal); 91.1g carbohydrate; 3.4g protein; 3.4g fibre*

Strawberries are easy to grow in the garden or on a balcony in a specially designed tiered pot. With the right soil, good sunlight and proper daily care, you can have a delicious crop year after year.

marshmallow pavlova

4 egg whites
1 cup (220g) caster sugar
½ teaspoon vanilla extract
¾ teaspoon white vinegar
300ml thickened cream, whipped
250g strawberries, halved

1 Preheat oven to 120°C/100°C fan-forced. Line oven tray with foil; grease foil, dust with cornflour, shake away excess. Mark 18cm-circle on foil.
2 Beat egg whites in small bowl with electric mixer until soft peaks form; gradually add sugar, beating until sugar dissolves. Add extract and vinegar; beat until combined.
3 Spread meringue into circle on foil, building up at the side to 8cm in height. Smooth side and top of pavlova gently. Using spatula blade, mark decorative grooves around side of pavlova; smooth top again.
4 Bake about 1½ hours. Turn off oven; cool pavlova in oven with door ajar. When pavlova is cold, cut around top edge (the crisp meringue top will fall slightly on top of the marshmallow). Top with cream and strawberries; dust with sifted icing sugar, if you like.
prep + cook time *1 hour 55 minutes (+ cooling)*
serves *8*
nutritional count per serving *14g total fat (9.2g saturated fat); 1078kJ (258 cal); 30g carbohydrate; 3.1g protein; 0.7g fibre*

patty cakes
with glacé icing

125g butter, softened
½ teaspoon vanilla extract
¾ cup (165g) caster sugar
3 eggs
2 cups (300g) self-raising flour
¼ cup (60ml) milk

glacé icing
2 cups (320g) icing sugar
20g butter, melted
2 tablespoons hot water, approximately

1 Preheat oven to 180°C/160°C fan-forced. Line a 12-hole (⅓-cup/80ml) muffin pan with paper cases.
2 Place ingredients in medium bowl; beat with electric mixer on low speed until ingredients are combined. Increase speed to medium; beat about 3 minutes or until mixture is smooth and paler in colour. Divide mixture among paper cases.
3 Bake cakes about 25 minutes. Stand cakes in pan 5 minutes before turning, top-side up, onto wire racks to cool.
4 Meanwhile, make glacé icing. Spread cool cakes with icing.
glacé icing Sift icing sugar into small heatproof bowl; stir in butter and enough of the water to make a firm paste. Stir over small saucepan of simmering water until icing is spreadable.
prep + cook time *45 minutes* **makes** *12*
nutritional count per cake *11.7g total fat (7.1g saturated fat); 1505kJ (360 cal); 58.3g carbohydrate; 4.4g protein; 1g fibre*

cake variations
berry & orange Stir in 1 teaspoon finely grated orange rind and ½ cup dried mixed berries at the end of step 2.
citrus Stir in ½ teaspoon each of finely grated lime, orange and lemon rind at the end of step 2.
passionfruit & white chocolate Stir in ¼ cup passionfruit pulp and ½ cup white Choc Bits at the end of step 2.

icing variations
coconut & lime Stir in ½ teaspoon coconut essence and 1 teaspoon finely grated lime rind.
orange Stir in 1 teaspoon finely grated orange rind. Replace 1 tablespoon of the hot water with orange juice.
passionfruit Stir in 1 tablespoon passionfruit pulp.

Passionfruit and pomegranate pulp will keep well when frozen. Prepare when the fruit is fresh and freeze immediately.

steamed ginger pudding

60g butter
¼ cup (90g) golden syrup
½ teaspoon bicarbonate of soda
1 cup (150g) self-raising flour
2 teaspoons ground ginger
½ cup (125ml) milk
1 egg

syrup
⅓ cup (115g) golden syrup
2 tablespoons water
30g butter

1 Grease 1.25-litre (5-cup) pudding steamer.
2 Stir butter and syrup in small saucepan over low heat until smooth. Remove from heat, stir in soda; transfer mixture to medium bowl. Stir in sifted dry ingredients then combined milk and egg, in two batches.
3 Spread mixture into steamer. Cover with pleated baking paper and foil; secure with lid.
4 Place pudding steamer in large saucepan with enough boiling water to come halfway up side of steamer; cover pan with tight-fitting lid. Boil 1 hour, replenishing water as necessary to maintain level. Stand pudding 5 minutes before turning onto plate.
5 Meanwhile, make syrup.
6 Serve pudding with syrup and, if you like, cream.
syrup Stir ingredients in small saucepan over heat until smooth; bring to the boil. Reduce heat; simmer, uncovered, 2 minutes.

prep + cook time *1 hour 15 minutes*   serves *6*
nutritional count per serving   *14.3g total fat (9g saturated fat); 1367kJ (327 cal); 44.5g carbohydrate; 4.5g protein; 1g fibre*

chocolate self-saucing pudding

60g butter
½ cup (125ml) milk
½ teaspoon vanilla extract
¾ cup (165g) caster sugar
1 cup (150g) self-raising flour
1 tablespoon cocoa powder
¾ cup (165g) firmly packed brown sugar
1 tablespoon cocoa powder, extra
2 cups (500ml) boiling water

1 Preheat oven to 180°C/160°C fan-forced. Grease 1.5-litre (6-cup) ovenproof dish.
2 Melt butter with milk in medium saucepan. Remove from heat; stir in extract and caster sugar then sifted flour and cocoa. Spread mixture into dish.
3 Sift brown sugar and extra cocoa over mixture; gently pour boiling water over mixture.
4 Bake pudding about 40 minutes or until centre is firm. Stand 5 minutes before serving.

prep + cook time *1 hour 5 minutes* serves *6*
nutritional count per serving *9.7g total fat (6.2g saturated fat); 1676kJ (401 cal); 73.4g carbohydrate; 3.8g protein; 1.1g fibre*

upside-down cake
with caramelised apple

2 large apples (400g)
60g unsalted butter, chopped
½ cup (110g) firmly packed brown sugar
1 teaspoon ground cinnamon
⅓ cup (50g) wholemeal self-raising flour
⅓ cup (80ml) low-fat milk
4 eggs, separated
¼ cup (55g) caster sugar
2 tablespoons flaked coconut

1 Preheat oven to 200°C/180°C fan-forced.
2 Peel and core apples; slice into 5mm rings.
3 Melt butter in heavy-based 25cm frying pan; add brown sugar and cinnamon; cook, stirring, until sugar dissolves. Remove from heat.
4 Place apple rings, overlapping slightly, on top of caramel in pan. Return to heat; cook, covered, over low heat, 2 minutes. Uncover; cook, over low heat, about 5 minutes or until apples are tender. Remove from heat.
5 Meanwhile, combine flour, milk and egg yolks in medium bowl.
6 Beat egg whites in small bowl with electric mixer until soft peaks form; gradually add caster sugar, beating until dissolved between additions. Fold egg white mixture into flour mixture, in two batches.
7 Spread mixture carefully over apple in pan. Bake, uncovered, in oven, about 12 minutes. Turn onto serving plate; serve sprinkled with coconut and, if you like, vanilla ice-cream.

prep + cook time *40 minutes*   serves *8*
nutritional count per serving   *10g total fat (5.8g saturated fat); 970kJ (232 cal); 28.9g carbohydrate; 4.9g protein; 1.7g fibre*

lamingtons

250g butter, softened
2 cups (440g) caster sugar
6 eggs
¾ cup (180g) sour cream
2 cups (300g) plain flour
¼ cup (35g) self-raising flour
2½ cups (200g) desiccated coconut

chocolate icing
4 cups (500g) icing sugar
½ cup (50g) cocoa powder
20g butter, melted
⅔ cup (160ml) milk

1 Preheat oven to 160°C/140°C fan-forced. Grease deep 23cm-square cake pan; line with baking paper.
2 Beat butter and sugar in large bowl with electric mixer until light and fluffy. Beat in eggs, one at a time. (Mixture might separate at this stage but will come together later.) Stir in sour cream and sifted flours, in two batches. Spread mixture into pan.
3 Bake cake about 55 minutes. Stand 10 minutes before turning, top-side up, onto wire rack to cool.
4 Meanwhile, make chocolate icing.
5 Trim cold cake so top is level; cut into 36 squares. Dip squares in icing, drain off excess then coat in coconut; place lamingtons on wire rack to set.
chocolate icing Sift icing sugar and cocoa into large heatproof bowl; stir in butter and milk. Stir icing over large saucepan of simmering water until it is of a coating consistency.
prep + cook time *2 hours 15 minutes (+ cooling)*
makes *36*
nutritional count per lamington *13.1g total fat (9.1g saturated fat); 1120kJ (268 cal); 33.9g carbohydrate; 3g protein; 1.2g fibre*

lemon delicious
pudding

125g butter, melted
2 teaspoons finely grated lemon rind
1½ cups (330g) caster sugar
3 eggs, separated
½ cup (75g) self-raising flour
⅓ cup (80ml) lemon juice
1⅓ cups (330ml) milk

1 Preheat oven to 180°C/160°C fan-forced. Grease six 1-cup (250ml) ovenproof dishes.
2 Combine butter, rind, sugar and yolks in large bowl. Stir in sifted flour then juice. Gradually stir in milk; mixture should be smooth and runny.
3 Beat egg whites in small bowl with electric mixer until soft peaks form; fold whites into lemon mixture, in two batches.
4 Place ovenproof dishes in large baking dish; divide lemon mixture among dishes. Add enough boiling water to baking dish to come halfway up sides of ovenproof dishes. Bake, uncovered, about 45 minutes.

prep + cook time *1 hour 5 minutes* **serves** *6*
nutritional count per serving *22g total fat (13.5g saturated fat); 2069kJ (495 cal); 67.1g carbohydrate; 6.7g protein; 0.5g fibre*

Rather than cooking all the cookie dough, stir some of the raw mixture through vanilla ice-cream for the ultimate cookie-dough ice-cream.

peanut butter
choc-chunk cookies

75g butter, softened
1 teaspoon vanilla extract
¼ cup (55g) caster sugar
¼ cup (55g) firmly packed brown sugar
⅔ cup (190g) smooth peanut butter
1 egg
1 cup (150g) plain flour
½ teaspoon bicarbonate of soda
150g milk eating chocolate, chopped coarsely

1 Preheat oven to 180°C/160°C fan-forced. Grease two oven trays; line with baking paper.
2 Beat butter, extract and sugars in small bowl with electric mixer until smooth. Add peanut butter; beat until combined. Add egg; beat until combined. Stir in sifted flour and soda, then chocolate.
3 Drop level tablespoons of mixture, about 5cm apart, onto trays; press down slightly to flatten.
4 Bake cookies about 10 minutes or until beginning to brown; cool on trays.

prep + cook time **25 minutes** makes **28**
nutritional count per cookie **7.3g total fat
(3g saturated fat); 531kJ (127 cal); 11.7g
carbohydrate; 3.1g protein; 1g fibre**

lemon meringue pie

½ cup (75g) cornflour
1 cup (220g) caster sugar
½ cup (125ml) lemon juice
1¼ cups (310ml) water
2 teaspoons finely grated lemon rind
60g unsalted butter, chopped
3 eggs, separated
½ cup (110g) caster sugar, extra

pastry
1½ cups (225g) plain flour
1 tablespoon icing sugar
140g cold butter, chopped
1 egg yolk
2 tablespoons cold water

1 Make pastry.
2 Grease 24cm-round loose-based fluted flan tin. Roll pastry between sheets of baking paper until large enough to line tin. Ease pastry into tin, press into base and side; trim edge. Cover; refrigerate 30 minutes.
3 Preheat oven to 240°C/220°C fan-forced.
4 Place tin on oven tray. Line pastry case with baking paper; fill with dried beans or rice. Bake 15 minutes; remove paper and beans carefully from pie shell. Bake about 10 minutes; cool pie shell, turn oven off.
5 Meanwhile, combine cornflour and sugar in medium saucepan; gradually stir in juice and the water until smooth. Cook, stirring, over high heat, until mixture boils and thickens. Reduce heat; simmer, stirring, 1 minute. Remove from heat; stir in rind, butter and egg yolks. Cool 10 minutes.
6 Spread filling into pie shell. Cover; refrigerate 2 hours.
7 Preheat oven to 240°C/220°C fan-forced.
8 Beat egg whites in small bowl with electric mixer until soft peaks form; gradually add extra sugar, beating until sugar dissolves.
9 Roughen surface of filling with fork, spread with meringue mixture. Bake about 2 minutes or until browned lightly.
pastry Process flour, icing sugar and butter until crumbly. Add egg yolk and the water; process until ingredients come together. Knead dough on floured surface until smooth. Cover; refrigerate 30 minutes.

prep + cook time *1 hour 5 minutes (+ refrigeration)*
serves *10*
nutritional count per serving *18.9g total fat (11.6g saturated fat); 1772kJ (424 cal); 57.7g carbohydrate; 5g protein; 0.9g fibre*

Unused egg whites can be frozen – place
one egg white per hole in an ice-cube tray.
Thaw before use in meringues and soufflés.

baked custard

6 eggs
1 teaspoon vanilla extract
⅓ cup (75g) caster sugar
1 litre (4 cups) hot milk
¼ teaspoon ground nutmeg

1 Preheat oven to 160°C/140°C fan-forced. Grease shallow 1.5-litre (6-cup) ovenproof dish.
2 Whisk eggs, extract and sugar in large bowl; gradually whisk in hot milk. Pour custard mixture into dish; sprinkle with nutmeg.
3 Place dish in larger baking dish; add enough boiling water to come halfway up sides of dish. Bake, uncovered, about 45 minutes. Remove custard from large dish; stand 5 minutes before serving.
prep + cook time *50 minutes* **serves** *6*
nutritional count per serving *11.8g total fat (5.9g saturated fat); 995kJ (238 cal); 20.7g carbohydrate; 12.3g protein; 0g fibre*

caramel tarts

18 (220g) butternut snap biscuits
395g can sweetened condensed milk
60g butter, chopped coarsely
⅓ cup (75g) firmly packed brown sugar
1 tablespoon lemon juice

1 Preheat oven to 160°C/140°C fan-forced. Grease two 12-hole (1½-tablespoons/30ml) shallow round-based patty pans.
2 Place one biscuit each over top of 18 pan holes. Bake about 4 minutes or until biscuits soften. Using the back of a teaspoon, gently press softened biscuits into pan holes; cool.
3 Stir condensed milk, butter and sugar in small heavy-based saucepan over heat until smooth. Bring to the boil; boil, stirring, about 10 minutes or until mixture is thick and dark caramel in colour. Remove from heat; stir in juice.
4 Divide mixture among biscuit cases; refrigerate 30 minutes or until set.
prep + cook time *35 minutes (+ refrigeration)*
makes *18*
nutritional count per tart *7.7g total fat (5g saturated fat); 727kJ (174 cal); 23.2g carbohydrate; 2.6g protein; 0.4g fibre*

Make your own health snacks using raisins, chopped nuts, dried bananas, apples and apricots. Your homemade snacks will contain less sugar than manufactured snack bars.

baked rice custard

4 eggs
⅓ cup (75g) caster sugar
½ teaspoon vanilla extract
2 cups (500ml) milk
300ml cream
⅓ cup (50g) raisins
1½ cups cold cooked white medium-grain rice
1 teaspoon ground cinnamon

1 Preheat oven to 180°C/160°C fan-forced. Grease 1.5-litre (6-cup) baking dish.
2 Whisk eggs, sugar and extract in medium bowl until combined. Whisk in milk and cream; stir in raisins and rice.
3 Pour mixture into dish. Place dish in large baking dish; pour enough boiling water into baking dish to come halfway up sides of dish. Bake 30 minutes, whisking lightly with fork under skin occasionally. Sprinkle with cinnamon; bake 20 minutes.
4 Serve rice custard warm or cold.
prep + cook time *1 hour*   serves *6*
nutritional count per serving *28.5g total fat (17.5g saturated fat); 1856kJ (444 cal); 37.3g carbohydrate; 9.5g protein; 0.8g fibre*

rice pudding

½ cup (100g) uncooked white medium-grain rice
2½ cups (625ml) milk
¼ cup (55g) caster sugar
¼ cup (40g) sultanas
½ teaspoon vanilla extract
2 teaspoons butter
½ teaspoon ground nutmeg

1 Preheat oven to 160°C/140°C fan-forced. Grease shallow 1-litre (4-cup) baking dish.
2 Wash rice under cold water; drain well. Combine rice, milk, sugar, sultanas and extract in dish; whisk lightly with fork. Dot with butter.
3 Bake pudding, uncovered, 1 hour, whisking lightly with fork under skin occasionally. Sprinkle with nutmeg; bake 20 minutes.
4 Serve rice pudding warm or cold.

prep + cook time *1 hour 30 minutes* **serves 6**
nutritional count per serving *5.5g total fat (3.6g saturated fat); 840kJ (201 cal); 32.4g carbohydrate; 4.8g protein; 0.4g fibre*

baked apples

4 large granny smith apples (800g)
50g butter, melted
⅓ cup (75g) firmly packed brown sugar
½ cup (80g) sultanas
1 teaspoon ground cinnamon

1 Preheat oven to 160°C/140°C fan-forced.
2 Core unpeeled apples about three-quarters of the way down from stem end, making hole 4cm in diameter. Use small sharp knife to score around centre of each apple.
3 Combine remaining ingredients in small bowl. Pack mixture firmly into apples; stand apples upright in small baking dish. Bake, uncovered, about 45 minutes.
prep + cook time *1 hour* serves *4*
nutritional count per serving *10.5g total fat (6.8g saturated fat); 1292kJ (309 cal); 50.2g carbohydrate; 1.2g protein; 4g fat*

variations
muesli filling Replace sultana mixture with ⅔ cup natural muesli, 1 cup thawed, well-drained frozen blueberries, 40g melted butter and 2 tablespoons brown sugar.
berry filling Replace sultana mixture with 1½ cups thawed well-drained frozen mixed berries. Bruise 4 cardamom pods; place one cardamom pod in each apple with mixed berries.

When apples are plentiful, make stewed apple and freeze it. You could also make apple juice – adding carrots and pears for more variety if you like. And apple sauce is a welcome store cupboard staple.

apple crumble

5 large apples (1kg)
¼ cup (55g) caster sugar
¼ cup (60ml) water

crumble
½ cup (75g) self-raising flour
¼ cup (35g) plain flour
½ cup (110g) firmly packed brown sugar
100g cold butter, chopped
1 teaspoon ground cinnamon

1 Preheat oven to 180°C/160°C fan-forced. Grease deep 1.5-litre (6-cup) baking dish.
2 Peel, core and quarter apples. Combine apple, sugar and the water in large saucepan; cook over low heat, covered, about 10 minutes. Drain; discard liquid.
3 Meanwhile, make crumble.
4 Place apples in dish; sprinkle with crumble. Bake about 25 minutes.
crumble Blend or process ingredients until combined.
prep + cook time *50 minutes* serves *4*
nutritional count per serving *21g total fat (13.6g saturated fat); 2245kJ (537 cal); 80.7g carbohydrate; 3.6g protein; 4.5g fat*

queen of puddings

2 cups (140g) stale breadcrumbs
1 tablespoon caster sugar
1 teaspoon vanilla extract
1 teaspoon finely grated lemon rind
2½ cups (625ml) milk
60g butter
4 eggs, separated
¼ cup (80g) raspberry jam, warmed
¾ cup (165g) caster sugar, extra

1 Preheat oven to 180°C/160°C fan-forced. Grease six ¾-cup (180ml) ovenproof dishes; stand on oven tray.
2 Combine breadcrumbs, sugar, extract and rind in large bowl. Heat milk and butter in medium saucepan until almost boiling, pour over bread mixture; stand 10 minutes. Stir in yolks. Divide mixture among dishes.
3 Bake pudding about 30 minutes. Carefully spread top of hot puddings with jam.
4 Beat egg whites in small bowl with electric mixer until soft peaks form; gradually add extra sugar, beating until sugar dissolves. Spoon meringue over puddings; bake about 10 minutes.

prep + cook time *1 hour* **serves** *6*
nutritional count per serving *16.6g total fat (9.3g saturated fat); 1843kJ (441 cal); 60.5g carbohydrate; 11.4g protein; 1.2g fibre*

crème caramel

¾ cup (165g) caster sugar
½ cup (125ml) water
300ml cream
1¾ cups (430ml) milk
6 eggs
1 teaspoon vanilla extract
⅓ cup (75g) caster sugar, extra

1 Preheat oven to 160°C/140°C fan-forced.
2 Stir sugar and the water in medium frying pan over heat, without boiling, until sugar dissolves. Bring to the boil; boil, uncovered, without stirring, until mixture is deep caramel in colour. Remove from heat; let bubbles subside. Pour into deep 20cm-round cake pan.
3 Combine cream and milk in medium saucepan; bring to the boil. Whisk eggs, extract and extra sugar in large bowl; whisking constantly, pour hot milk mixture into egg mixture. Strain mixture into cake pan.
4 Place pan in medium baking dish; add enough boiling water to come half way up side of pan. Bake, uncovered, about 40 minutes or until firm. Remove custard from baking dish, cover; refrigerate overnight.
5 Gently ease crème caramel from side of pan; invert onto deep-sided serving plate.

prep + cook time *1 hour (+ refrigeration)* serves *6*
nutritional count per serving *29.7g total fat (17.7g saturated fat); 2031kJ (486 cal); 45g carbohydrate; 10.1g protein; 0g fibre*

Buy nuts, seeds and dried fruits in bulk from a reputable health store. Store in airtight containers in a cool place.

cinnamon almond cake

¼ cup (40g) roasted almonds
½ cup (125ml) milk
80g butter, softened
1 teaspoon vanilla extract
½ cup (110g) firmly packed brown sugar
2 eggs
1 cup (150g) self-raising flour
2 teaspoons ground cinnamon
20g butter, melted

nut topping
½ cup (80g) blanched almonds, chopped finely
¼ cup (40g) icing sugar
1 teaspoon ground cinnamon

1 Preheat oven to 180°C/160°C fan-forced. Grease 8cm x 26cm bar cake pan; line base with baking paper, extending paper 5cm above long sides of pan.
2 Blend or process nuts until chopped coarsely; add milk, process until smooth.
3 Beat softened butter, extract and sugar in small bowl with electric mixer until light and fluffy. Beat in eggs, one at a time. (Mixture may separate at this stage, but will come together later.) Stir in sifted flour, cinnamon and almond mixture. Pour mixture into pan.
4 Bake cake about 35 minutes. Stand cake in pan 10 minutes before turning, top-side up, onto wire rack to cool.
5 Increase temperature to 200°C/180°C fan-forced.
6 Meanwhile, make nut topping.
7 Brush cake with melted butter; sprinkle with nut topping.

nut topping Place nuts in strainer; rinse under cold water. Combine wet nuts in small bowl with sifted icing sugar and cinnamon; spread mixture onto oven tray, roast about 10 minutes or until nuts are dry.

prep + cook time *55 minutes*   **serves** *6*
nutritional count per serving *27.7g total fat (10.8g saturated fat); 1956kJ (468 cal); 44g carbohydrate; 9.6g protein; 2.8g fibre*

Buy cheaper, day-old bakery items when you need cake to use as a base for trifles and summer fruit puddings or bread to make breadcrumbs.

classic trifle

85g packet raspberry jelly crystals
250g sponge cake, cut into 3cm pieces
¼ cup (60ml) sweet sherry
¼ cup (30g) custard powder
¼ cup (55g) caster sugar
½ teaspoon vanilla extract
1½ cups (375ml) milk
825g can sliced peaches, drained
300ml thickened cream
2 tablespoons flaked almonds, roasted

1 Make jelly according to directions on packet; pour into shallow container. Refrigerate 20 minutes or until jelly is almost set.
2 Arrange cake in 3-litre (12-cup) bowl; sprinkle with sherry.
3 Blend custard powder, sugar and extract with a little of the milk in small saucepan; stir in remaining milk. Stir over heat until mixture boils and thickens. Cover surface with plastic wrap; cool.
4 Pour jelly over cake; refrigerate 15 minutes. Top with peaches. Stir a third of the cream into custard; pour over peaches.
5 Whip remaining cream; spread over custard, sprinkle with nuts. Refrigerate 3 hours or overnight.
prep + cook time *40 minutes (+ refrigeration)*
serves *8*
nutritional count per serving *16.7g total fat (10.9g saturated fat); 1689kJ (404 cal); 47g carbohydrate; 7.1g protein; 1.6g fat*

Preserve soft fruits such as peaches and apricots when they are in season so you can enjoy them in winter. Fresh from the fruit market or from the local orchard, these are fruits to treasure out of season.

impossible pie

You'll discover when you make this pie how it got its name: when cooked, the pie magically separates into three perfect layers. Impossible!

½ cup (75g) plain flour
1 cup (220g) caster sugar
¾ cup (60g) desiccated coconut
4 eggs
1 teaspoon vanilla extract
125g butter, melted
½ cup (40g) flaked almonds
2 cups (500ml) milk

1 Preheat oven to 180°C/160°C fan-forced. Grease deep 24cm pie dish.
2 Combine sifted flour, sugar, coconut, eggs, extract, butter and half the nuts in large bowl; gradually add milk, stirring, until combined. Pour mixture into dish.
3 Bake pie 35 minutes. Remove pie from oven, sprinkle with remaining nuts; bake 10 minutes.
4 Serve pie with cream or fruit, if you like.
prep + cook time *55 minutes*   serves *8*
nutritional count per serving *25.7g total fat (15.4g saturated fat); 1747kJ (418 cal); 38.2g carbohydrate; 8.1g protein; 1.9g fat*

frozen green apple yogurt

⅓ cup (115g) honey
½ cup (125ml) apple juice
1 teaspoon gelatine
¾ cup (130g) finely grated unpeeled apple
500g greek-style yogurt
1 tablespoon passionfruit pulp

1 Stir honey and juice in small saucepan over low heat until honey melts; cool syrup 5 minutes.
2 Sprinkle gelatine over syrup; stir until gelatine dissolves.
3 Combine gelatine mixture, apple and yogurt in 14cm x 21cm loaf pan. Cover with foil; freeze 3 hours or overnight.
4 Remove yogurt from freezer 15 minutes before serving; top each serving with pulp.

pre + cook time *20 minutes (+ freezing)* serves *4*
nutritional count per serving *4.3g total fat (2.8g saturated fat); 932kJ (223 cal); 37.4g carbohydrate; 7g protein; 2g fibre*

variations

mango Substitute water for the juice in syrup; substitute 300g thawed coarsely chopped frozen mango for the apple.

raspberry Substitute water for the juice in syrup; substitute 150g thawed frozen raspberries for the apple. Push thawed raspberries through a fine sieve over small bowl; discard seeds.

Buy tropical fruits such as mango, in bulk, when they are in season – peel, then freeze the flesh. Fresh berries such as blueberries, blackberries and boysenberries can also be frozen for use out of season.

These breads make a delicious breakfast in a flash – pop a slice or two under the grill for a couple of minutes until it begins to brown then, if you like, spread with butter. They also freeze well – slice the whole loaf, wrap it well in plastic wrap and freeze in an air-tight container; thaw or toast as needed.

coconut bread

1 cup (150g) plain flour
½ cup (75g) self-raising flour
1 cup (220g) caster sugar
⅔ cup (50g) desiccated coconut
75g butter, melted
2 eggs, beaten lightly
1 teaspoon coconut extract
1 cup (250ml) buttermilk

1 Preheat oven to 180°C/160°C fan-forced. Grease 14cm x 21cm loaf pan; line base with baking paper, extending paper 5cm above long sides of pan.
2 Sift flours into medium bowl; stir in sugar and coconut.
3 Add butter, egg, extract and buttermilk to flour mixture, stir until combined; pour into pan.
4 Bake about 1 hour. Stand loaf in pan 10 minutes before turning, top-side up, onto wire rack to cool.
prep + cook time *1 hour 10 minutes*   **serves** *8*
nutritional count per serving *14.1g total fat (9.5g saturated fat); 1492kJ (357 cal); 49.9g carbohydrate; 6.4g protein; 2g fibre*

banana bread

You need two large overripe bananas (460g) for this recipe.

90g unsalted butter, softened
1 teaspoon vanilla extract
1 cup (220g) firmly packed brown sugar
2 eggs
1 cup mashed banana
1 cup (150g) plain flour
1 cup (150g) self-raising flour

1 Preheat oven to 180°C/160°C fan-forced. Grease 14cm x 21cm loaf pan; line base and long sides with baking paper, extending paper 5cm above long sides.
2 Beat butter, extract and sugar in small bowl with electric mixer until light and fluffy. Beat in eggs, one at a time. Transfer mixture to large bowl; stir in banana then sifted flours, in two batches. Spread mixture into pan; cover with a strip of pleated foil.
3 Bake bread 40 minutes; uncover, bake about 30 minutes. Stand 5 minutes; lift onto wire rack to cool. Serve toasted or warm, with butter if you like.
prep + cook time *1 hour 20 minutes*   makes *12 slices*
nutritional count per slice *9.5g total fat (5.6g saturated fat); 1296kJ (309 cal); 49.7g carbohydrate; 5.1g protein; 1.7g fibre*

glossary

ALLSPICE also called pimento or jamaican pepper; tastes like a combination of nutmeg, cumin, clove and cinnamon. Available whole or ground.

ALMONDS
blanched brown skins removed.
flaked paper-thin slices.
slivered small pieces cut lengthways.

BACON also known as bacon slices.

BARLEY a nutritious grain used in soups and stews. Hulled barley, the least processed, is high in fibre. Pearl barley has had the husk removed then been steamed and polished so that only the "pearl" of the original grain remains, much the same as white rice.

BASIL
sweet the most common type of basil; used extensively in Italian dishes and one of the main ingredients in pesto.
thai also known as horapa; different from holy basil and sweet basil in both look and taste, having smaller leaves and purplish stems. It has a slight aniseed taste.

BAY LEAVES aromatic leaves from the bay tree available fresh or dried; adds a strong, slightly peppery flavour.

BEANS
black-eyed also called black-eyed peas or cowpea; the dried seed of a variant of the snake or yard-long bean. Not too dissimilar to white beans in flavour.
borlotti also called roman beans or pink beans, can be eaten fresh or dried. Interchangeable with pinto beans due to their similarity in appearance – pale pink or beige with dark red streaks.
broad also called fava, windsor and horse beans; available dried, fresh, canned and frozen. Fresh should be peeled twice (discarding both the outer long green pod and the beige-green tough inner shell); the frozen beans have had their pods removed but the beige shell still needs removal.
cannellini small white bean similar in appearance and flavour to other *phaseolus vulgaris* varieties (great

northern, navy or haricot). Available dried or canned.
green also known as french or string beans (although the tough string they once had has generally been bred out of them), this long thin fresh bean is consumed in its entirety once cooked.
kidney medium-size red bean, slightly floury in texture yet sweet in flavour; sold dried or canned, it's found in bean mixes and is used in chilli con carne.
refried pinto or borlotti beans, cooked twice: first soaked and boiled, then mashed and fried (traditionally in lard). A Mexican staple, frijoles refritos (refried beans) are sold canned in supermarkets.
white a generic term we use for canned or dried cannellini, haricot, navy or great northern beans.

BEETROOT also known as red beets.

BICARBONATE OF SODA also known as baking soda.

BREADCRUMBS
packaged prepared fine-textured but crunchy white breadcrumbs; good for coating foods that are to be fried.
stale crumbs made by grating, blending or processing 1- or 2-day-old bread.

BUK CHOY also known as bok choy, pak choi, Chinese white cabbage or Chinese chard; has a fresh, mild mustard taste. Use stems and leaves, stir-fried or braised. Baby buk choy, also known as pak kat farang or shanghai bok choy, is much smaller and more tender. Its mildly acrid, distinctively appealing taste has made it one of the most commonly used Asian greens.

BUTTER we use salted butter unless stated otherwise; 125g is equal to 1 stick (4 ounces).

CAPERS the grey-green buds of a warm climate (usually Mediterranean) shrub, sold either dried and salted or pickled in a vinegar brine; tiny young ones, called baby capers, are also available both in brine or dried in salt. Their pungent taste adds piquancy to a tapenade, sauces and condiments.

CAPSICUM also called pepper or bell pepper. Discard seeds and membranes before use.

CARAWAY SEEDS the small, half-moon-shaped dried seed from a member of the parsley family; adds a sharp anise flavour when used in both sweet and savoury dishes. Used widely, in foods such as rye bread, harissa and the classic Hungarian fresh cheese, liptauer.

CARDAMOM a spice native to India and used extensively in its cuisine; can be purchased in pod, seed or ground form. Has a distinctive aromatic, sweetly rich flavour and is one of the world's most expensive spices.

CAYENNE PEPPER a thin-fleshed, long, extremely hot dried red chilli, usually purchased ground.

CELERIAC tuberous root with knobbly brown skin, white flesh and a celery-like flavour. Keep peeled celeriac in acidulated water to stop it discolouring. It can be grated and eaten raw in salads; used in soups and stews; boiled and mashed like potatoes; or sliced thinly and deep-fried as chips.

CHEESE
bocconcini from the diminutive of "boccone", meaning mouthful in Italian; walnut-sized, baby mozzarella, a delicate, semi-soft, white cheese traditionally made from buffalo milk. Sold fresh, it spoils rapidly so will only keep, refrigerated in brine, for 1 or 2 days at the most.
cream cheese commonly called philly or philadelphia; a soft cow-milk cheese.
fetta Greek in origin; a crumbly textured goat- or sheep-milk cheese having a sharp, salty taste. Ripened and stored in salted whey.
goats made from goat milk, has an earthy, strong taste. Available in soft, crumbly and firm textures, in various shapes and sizes, and sometimes rolled in ash or herbs.
gruyère a hard-rind Swiss cheese with small holes and a nutty, slightly salty flavour. A popular cheese for soufflés.

mozzarella soft, spun-curd cheese. Has a low melting point and elastic texture; is used to add texture rather than flavour.

parmesan also known as parmigiano; is a hard, grainy cow-milk cheese. The curd is salted in brine for a month, then aged for up to 2 years.

pecorino the Italian generic name for cheeses made from sheep milk. This family of hard, white to pale-yellow cheeses, traditionally made in the Italian winter and spring, have been matured for 8 to 12 months. They are classified according to the area in which they were produced – romano from Rome, sardo from Sardinia, siciliano from Sicily and toscano from Tuscany. If you can't find it, use parmesan.

pizza cheese a commercial blend of varying proportions of processed grated mozzarella, cheddar and parmesan.

ricotta a sweet, moist, soft, white, cows-milk cheese; has a slightly grainy texture.

CHICKPEAS also called garbanzos, hummus or channa; an irregularly round, sandy-coloured legume used extensively in Mediterranean, Indian and Hispanic cooking. Firm texture even after cooking, a floury mouth-feel and robust nutty flavour; available canned or dried (reconstitute for several hours in cold water before use).

CHILLI use rubber gloves when seeding and chopping fresh chillies as they can burn your skin. We use unseeded chillies because the seeds contain the heat; use fewer chillies rather than seeding the lot.

flakes also sold as crushed chilli; dehydrated deep-red extremely fine slices and whole seeds.

jalapeño pronounced hah-lah-pain-yo. Fairly hot, medium-sized, plump, dark green chilli; available pickled, sold canned or bottled, and fresh, from greengrocers.

powder the Asian variety is the hottest, made from dried ground thai chillies; can be used instead of fresh in the proportion of ½ teaspoon chilli powder to 1 medium chopped fresh red chilli.

red thai also known as "scuds"; tiny, very hot and bright red in colour.

CHINESE COOKING WINE also called hao hsing or chinese rice wine; made from fermented rice, wheat, sugar and salt with a 13.5 per cent alcohol content. Inexpensive and found in Asian food shops; if you can't find it, replace with mirin or sherry.

CHOCOLATE

Choc Bits also known as chocolate chips or chocolate morsels; available in milk, white and dark chocolate. Made of cocoa liquor, cocoa butter, sugar and an emulsifier, these hold their shape in baking and are ideal for decorating.

dark eating also known as semi-sweet or luxury chocolate; made of a high percentage of cocoa liquor and cocoa butter, and little added sugar. Unless stated otherwise, we use dark eating chocolate in this book as it's ideal for use in desserts and cakes.

milk eating most popular eating chocolate, mild and very sweet; similar in make-up to dark with the difference being the addition of milk solids.

white contains no cocoa solids but derives its sweet flavour from cocoa butter. Very sensitive to heat.

CINNAMON available both in the piece (called sticks or quills) and ground into powder; one of the world's most common spices, used universally as a sweet, fragrant flavouring for both sweet and savoury foods. The dried inner bark of the shoots of the Sri Lankan native cinnamon tree; much of what is sold as the real thing is in fact cassia, Chinese cinnamon, from the bark of the cassia tree. Less expensive to process than true cinnamon, it is often blended with Sri Lankan cinnamon to produce the type of "cinnamon" most commonly found in supermarkets.

CLOVES dried flower buds of a tropical tree; can be used whole or in ground form. They have a strong scent and taste so should be used sparingly.

COCOA POWDER also known as unsweetened cocoa; cocoa beans (cacao seeds) that have been fermented, roasted, shelled, ground into powder then cleared of most of the fat content.

COCONUT

cream obtained commercially from the first pressing of the coconut flesh alone, without the addition of water; the second pressing (less rich) is sold as coconut milk. Available in cans and cartons at most supermarkets.

desiccated concentrated, dried, unsweetened and finely shredded coconut flesh.

flaked dried flaked coconut flesh.

milk not the liquid found inside the fruit, which is called coconut water, but the diluted liquid from the second pressing of the white flesh of a mature coconut (the first pressing produces coconut cream). Available in cans and cartons at most supermarkets.

CORIANDER also called cilantro, pak chee or chinese parsley; a bright-green-leafed herb having both pungent aroma and taste. The stems and roots of the herb are used in Thai cooking; wash well before chopping. Also available ground or as seeds; these should not be substituted for fresh coriander as the tastes are completely different.

CORNFLOUR also known as cornstarch. Made from corn or wheat and used as a thickening agent in cooking.

CORNICHONS French for gherkin, a very small variety of cucumber. Pickled, they are a traditional accompaniment to pâté; the Swiss always serve them with fondue (or raclette).

COUSCOUS a fine, grain-like cereal product made from semolina; from the countries of North Africa. A semolina flour and water dough is sieved then dehydrated to produce minuscule even-sized pellets of couscous; it is rehydrated by steaming or with the addition of a warm liquid and swells to three or four times its original size.

CUMIN also known as zeera or comino; has a spicy, nutty flavour. Available in seed, dried and ground forms.

CURRY PASTES are available in various strengths in many supermarkets; adjust the amount to suit your palate.

CURRY POWDER a blend of ground spices (dried chilli, cinnamon, coriander, cumin, fennel, fenugreek, cardamom, mace, tumeric). Available mild or hot.

CUSTARD POWDER instant mixture used to make pouring custard; similar to North American instant pudding mixes.

EGGPLANT also called aubergine.

FISH SAUCE called naam pla (Thai) or nuoc naam (Vietnamese); the two are almost identical. Made from pulverised salted fermented fish (anchovies); has a pungent smell and strong taste. Available in varying degrees of intensity, so use according to taste.

FLOUR
plain also known as all-purpose.
self-raising all-purpose plain or wholemeal flour with baking powder and salt added; make yourself in the proportion of 1 cup plain flour to 2 teaspoons baking powder.
wholemeal also known as wholewheat flour; milled with the wheat germ so is higher in fibre and more nutritional than plain flour.

GALANGAL also known as ka or lengkaus if fresh and laos if dried and powdered; a root, similar to ginger in its use. It has a hot-sour ginger-citrusy flavour; used in fish curries and soups.

GARAM MASALA literally meaning blended spices in its northern Indian place of origin; based on varying proportions of cardamom, cinnamon, cloves, coriander, fennel and cumin, roasted and ground together. Black pepper and chilli can be added for a hotter version.

GELATINE we use dried (powdered) gelatine in this book; it's also available in sheet form known as leaf gelatine.

GHEE clarified butter; with the milk solids removed, this fat has a high smoking point so can be heated to a high temperature without burning.

GINGER
fresh also called green or root ginger; the thick gnarled root of a tropical plant. Can be kept, peeled, covered with dry sherry in a jar and refrigerated, or frozen in an airtight container.
glacé fresh ginger root preserved in sugar syrup.
ground also called powdered ginger; used as a flavouring in baking but cannot be substituted for fresh ginger.

GOLDEN SYRUP a by-product of refined sugarcane; pure maple syrup or honey can be substituted. Golden syrup and treacle (a thicker, darker syrup not unlike molasses), also known as flavour syrups, are similar sugar products made by partly breaking down sugar into its component parts and adding water. Treacle is more viscous, and has a stronger flavour and aroma than golden syrup (which has been refined further and contains fewer impurities, so is lighter in colour and more fluid). Both can be use in baking and for making certain confectionery items.

HARISSA a North African paste made from dried red chillies, garlic, olive oil and caraway seeds; can be used as a rub for meat, an ingredient in sauces and dressings, or eaten as a condiment. It is available from Middle Eastern food shops and some supermarkets.

HOISIN SAUCE a thick, sweet and spicy Chinese barbecue sauce made from salted fermented soybeans, onions and garlic; used as a marinade or baste, or to accent stir-fries and barbecued or roasted foods. From Asian food shops and supermarkets.

KAFFIR LIME LEAVES also known as bai magrood and looks like two glossy dark green leaves joined end to end, forming a rounded hourglass shape. Used fresh or dried in many South-East Asian dishes, they are used like bay leaves or curry leaves, especially in Thai cooking. Sold fresh, dried or frozen, the dried leaves are less potent so double the number if using them as a substitute for fresh; a strip of fresh lime peel may be substituted for each kaffir lime leaf.

KECAP ASIN is an astringent, salty soy sauce native to the cooking of Indonesia; available from Asian food stores.

KUMARA the polynesian name of an orange-fleshed sweet potato often confused with yam; good baked, boiled, mashed or fried like other potatoes.

LEBANESE CUCUMBERS short, slender and thin-skinned. Probably the most popular variety because of its tender, edible skin, tiny, yielding seeds, and sweet, fresh and flavoursome taste.

LEMON GRASS a tall, clumping, lemon-smelling and -tasting, sharp-edged grass; the white lower part of the stem is used, chopped, in Asian cooking.

LENTILS (red, brown, yellow) dried pulses often identified by and named after their colour. Eaten by cultures all over the world, most famously perhaps in the dhals of India, lentils have high food value.
green (australian fine or french green) a local cousin to the famous (and very expensive) French lentils du puy; green-blue, tiny lentils with a nutty, earthy flavour and a hardy nature that allows them to be rapidly cooked without disintegrating.

MAPLE SYRUP a thin syrup distilled from the sap of the maple tree. Maple-flavoured syrup or pancake syrup is not an adequate substitute for the real thing.

MILK we use full-cream homogenised milk unless otherwise specified.
buttermilk in spite of its name, buttermilk is actually low in fat, varying between 0.6 per cent and 2.0 per cent per 100ml. Originally the term given to the slightly sour liquid left after butter was churned from cream, today it is intentionally made from no-fat or low-fat milk to which specific bacterial cultures have been added during the manufacturing process. It is readily available from the dairy department in supermarkets.
sweetened condensed a canned milk product consisting of milk with more than half the water content removed and sugar added to the remaining milk.

MUSHROOMS
button small, cultivated white mushrooms with a mild flavour.
swiss brown also known as roman or cremini. Light to dark brown mushrooms with full-bodied flavour; suited for use in casseroles or being stuffed and baked.

MUSTARD
dijon also called french. Pale brown, creamy, distinctively flavoured, fairly mild French mustard.
english traditional hot, pungent, deep yellow mustard. Serve with roast beef and ham; wonderful with hard cheeses.
wholegrain also known as seeded. A French-style coarse-grain mustard made from crushed mustard seeds and dijon-style french mustard. Works well with cold meats and sausages.

MUSTARD SEEDS
black also known as brown mustard seeds; more pungent than the white variety; used frequently in curries.
white also known as yellow mustard seeds; used ground for mustard powder and in most prepared mustards.

NUTMEG a strong and pungent spice ground from the dried nut of an evergreen tree native to Indonesia. Usually found ground but the flavour is more intense from a whole nut, available from spice shops, so it's best to grate your own. Used most often in baking and milk-based desserts, but also works nicely in savoury dishes. Found in mixed spice mixtures.

OIL
cooking spray we use a cholesterol-free cooking spray made from canola oil.
olive made from ripened olives. Extra virgin and virgin are the first and second press, respectively, of the olives and are therefore considered the best; the "extra light" or "light" name on other types refers to taste not fat levels.
peanut pressed from ground peanuts; the most commonly used oil in Asian cooking because of its high capacity to handle high heat without burning.
vegetable any oil sourced from plant rather than animal fats.

ONION
fried onion/shallots served as a condiment on Asian tables to be sprinkled over just-cooked food. Found in cellophane bags or jars at all Asian grocery shops; once opened, they will keep for months if stored tightly sealed.
green also known as scallion or (incorrectly) shallot; an immature onion picked before the bulb has formed, having a long, bright-green edible stalk.
red also known as spanish, red spanish or bermuda onion; a sweet-flavoured, large, purple-red onion.

PANCETTA an Italian unsmoked bacon; pork belly cured in salt and spices then rolled into a sausage shape and dried for several weeks.

PAPRIKA ground dried sweet red capsicum (bell pepper); there are many grades and types available, including sweet, hot, mild and smoked.

PINE NUTS also known as pignoli; not a nut but a small, cream-coloured kernel from pine cones. They are best roasted before use to bring out the flavour.

POLENTA also known as cornmeal; a flour-like cereal made of dried corn (maize). Also the dish made from it.

POTATOES
coliban round, smooth white skin and flesh; good for baking and mashing.
king edward slightly plump and rosy; great mashed.
lasoda round, red skin with deep eyes, white flesh; good for mashing or roasting.
russet burbank long and oval, rough white skin with shallow eyes, white flesh; good for baking and frying.
sebago white skin, oval; good fried, mashed and baked.

PRESERVED LEMON whole or quartered salted lemons preserved in a mixture of olive oil and lemon juice; a North African specialty, they are usually added to casseroles and tagines to impart a rich, salty-sour acidic flavour. Available from delicatessens and specialty food shops. Use the rind only and rise well under cold water before using.

RICE
arborio small, round grain rice well-suited to absorb a large amount of liquid; the high level of starch makes it especially suitable for risottos, giving the dish its classic creaminess.
jasmine a long-grained white rice recognised around the world as having a perfumed aromatic quality; moist in texture, it clings together after cooking. Sometimes substituted for basmati rice.
RISONI small rice-shape pasta; very similar to another small pasta, orzo.

ROCKET also called arugula, rugula and rucola; peppery green leaf eaten raw in salads or used in cooking. Baby rocket leaves are smaller and less peppery.

SAFFRON stigma of a member of the crocus family, available ground or in strands; imparts a yellow-orange colour to food once infused. The quality can vary greatly; the best is the most expensive spice in the world.

SAUSAGES
chorizo sausage of Spanish origin, made of coarsely ground pork and highly seasoned with garlic and chilli.
merguez a small, spicy sausage believed to have originated in Tunisia but eaten throughout North Africa, France and Spain; is traditionally made with lamb meat and is easily recognised because of its chilli-red colour. Available from many butchers, delicatessens and specialty sausage stores.

SAVOY CABBAGE large, heavy head with crinkled dark-green outer leaves; a fairly mild tasting cabbage.

SHALLOTS also called french shallots, golden shallots or eschalots. Small and elongated, with a brown-skin, they grow in tight clusters similar to garlic.

SILVER BEET also known as Swiss chard and incorrectly, spinach; has fleshy stalks and large leaves, both of which can be prepared as for spinach.

SOY SAUCE also known as sieu; made from fermented soybeans. Several variations are available in supermarkets and Asian food stores; we use Japanese soy sauce unless indicated otherwise.

SPINACH also known as english spinach and incorrectly, silver beet. Baby spinach

leaves are best eaten raw in salads; the larger leaves should be added last to soups, stews and stir-fries, and should be cooked until barely wilted.

STAR ANISE a dried star-shaped pod whose seeds have an astringent aniseed flavour; commonly used to flavour stocks and marinades.

SUGAR
brown a soft, finely granulated sugar retaining molasses for colour and flavour.
caster also known as superfine or finely granulated table sugar.
icing also known as confectioners' sugar or powdered sugar; pulverised granulated sugar crushed together with a small amount of cornflour.
palm also called nam tan pip, jaggery, jawa or gula melaka; made from the sap of the sugar palm tree. Light brown to black in colour and usually sold in rock-hard cakes; use brown sugar if unavailable.
white a coarse, granulated table sugar, also known as crystal sugar.

TAMARIND CONCENTRATE (or paste) the commercial result of the distillation of tamarind juice into a condensed, compacted paste.

TURMERIC also called kamin; is a rhizome related to galangal and ginger. Must be grated or pounded to release its acrid aroma and pungent flavour. Known for the golden colour it imparts, fresh turmeric can be substituted with the more commonly found dried powder.

VANILLA EXTRACT obtained from vanilla beans infused in water; a non-alcoholic version of essence.

VINEGAR
balsamic originally from Modena, Italy, there are now many balsamic vinegars on the market ranging in pungency and quality depending on how, and for how long, they have been aged. Quality can be determined up to a point by price; use the most expensive sparingly.
cider made from fermented apples.

WATERCRESS one of the cress family, a large group of peppery greens used raw in salads, dips and sandwiches, or cooked in soups. Highly perishable, so it must be used as soon as possible after purchase.

WORCESTERSHIRE SAUCE thin, dark-brown spicy sauce developed by the British when in India; used as a seasoning for meat, gravies and cocktails, and as a condiment.

YOGURT we use plain full-cream yogurt unless stated otherwise.

ZUCCHINI also known as courgette.

conversion chart

MEASURES

One Australian metric measuring cup holds approximately 250ml; one Australian metric tablespoon holds 20ml; one Australian metric teaspoon holds 5ml.

The difference between one country's measuring cups and another's is within a two- or three-teaspoon variance, and will not affect your cooking results. North America, New Zealand and the United Kingdom use a 15ml tablespoon.

All cup and spoon measurements are level. The most accurate way of measuring dry ingredients is to weigh them. When measuring liquids, use a clear glass or plastic jug with the metric markings.

We use large eggs with an average weight of 60g.

DRY MEASURES

METRIC	IMPERIAL
15g	½oz
30g	1oz
60g	2oz
90g	3oz
125g	4oz (¼lb)
155g	5oz
185g	6oz
220g	7oz
250g	8oz (½lb)
280g	9oz
315g	10oz
345g	11oz
375g	12oz (¾lb)
410g	13oz
440g	14oz
470g	15oz
500g	16oz (1lb)
750g	24oz (1½lb)
1kg	32oz (2lb)

LIQUID MEASURES

METRIC	IMPERIAL
30ml	1 fluid oz
60ml	2 fluid oz
100ml	3 fluid oz
125ml	4 fluid oz
150ml	5 fluid oz (¼ pint/1 gill)
190ml	6 fluid oz
250ml	8 fluid oz
300ml	10 fluid oz (½ pint)
500ml	16 fluid oz
600ml	20 fluid oz (1 pint)
1000ml (1 litre)	1¾ pints

LENGTH MEASURES

METRIC	IMPERIAL
3mm	⅛in
6mm	¼in
1cm	½in
2cm	¾in
2.5cm	1in
5cm	2in
6cm	2½in
8cm	3in
10cm	4in
13cm	5in
15cm	6in
18cm	7in
20cm	8in
23cm	9in
25cm	10in
28cm	11in
30cm	12in (1ft)

OVEN TEMPERATURES

These oven temperatures are only a guide for conventional ovens. For fan-forced ovens, check the manufacturer's manual.

	°C (CELSIUS)	°F (FAHRENHEIT)	GAS MARK
Very slow	120	250	½
Slow	150	275-300	1-2
Moderately slow	160	325	3
Moderate	180	350-375	4-5
Moderately hot	200	400	6
Hot	220	425-450	7-8
Very hot	240	475	9

index